SURVIVING AN
EATING DISORDER

FOURTH REVISED EDITION

SURVIVING AN EATING DISORDER

FOURTH REVISED EDITION

Strategies for Family and Friends

MICHELE SIEGEL, PhD

JUDITH BRISMAN, PhD, CEDS

MARGOT WEINSHEL, LCSW

HARPER PERENNIAL

NEW YORK • LONDON • TORONTO • SYDNEY • NEW DELHI • AUCKLAND

HARPER ● PERENNIAL

Originally published in 1988 by Harper & Row, an imprint of HarperCollins Publishers.

SURVIVING AN EATING DISORDER, FOURTH REVISED EDITION. Copyright © 1988, 1997, 2009, 2021 by Judith Brisman, Margot Weinshel, Jesse Barocas and Josh Barocas (as successors in interest to Michele Siegel). All rights reserved. Printed in the United States of America. No part of this book may be used or reproduced in any manner whatsoever without written permission except in the case of brief quotations embodied in critical articles and reviews. For information, address HarperCollins Publishers, 195 Broadway, New York, NY 10007.

HarperCollins books may be purchased for educational, business, or sales promotional use. For information, please email the Special Markets Department at SPsales@harpercollins.com.

FIRST COLLINS LIVING EDITION PUBLISHED 2009.

FIRST HARPER PERENNIAL EDITION PUBLISHED 2021.

Designed by Jamie Lynn Kerner

Library of Congress Cataloging-in-Publication Data has been applied for.

ISBN 978-0-06-295414-5

21 22 23 24 25 LSC 10 9 8 7 6 5 4 3 2 1

To our patients and their families, who, in their willingness to share their struggles, have asked us the questions and taught us the answers

Contents

PART III: USING NEW STRATEGIES 181

Acknowledgments

ONE ONLY CAN HOPE THAT IT IS POSSIBLE TO CHANGE THE WORLD BY virtue of having lived a life. Michele Siegel lived a life filled with joy, spirit, and a laughter that embraced everyone around her. She also knew that the families we treated had been somehow lost in the mix and she worked hard to change that. *Surviving* was Michele's idea and, for each family supported by this book, we want to acknowledge Michele for her inspiration from the start.

Frances Goldin changed the world daily with an ever-present sense of dignity, fight, and quiet persistence (sometimes not so quiet!). Our first agent, Frances fought for this book's stability and in that sense allowed *Surviving* to come alive. With Frances' passing, the world has lost one of the fiercest advocates for change. We will miss her. Ellen Geiger continued in Frances' role as our agent. Without Ellen's tenacity and patience, *Surviving* would surely have come to a full stop.

Our editor, Sarah Stein, allowed us the freedom to bring new ideas and sensibilities to this edition while keeping us steady in the needed boundaries of time. And our copy editor, Christina Verigan, brought an exquisite appreciation of language to translate our often flat-footed words into readable thoughts.

I am grateful to my parents, Jerome and Gloria Brisman, and my three brothers who ever reminded me that "going home" could be a haven of safety and joy. And most especially to my daughters, Julia and Senna Lauer, who have filled my life with laughter and love and have taught me more than any training program could possibly allow.

Thanks to Robert and Stephanie Bazell for their love and support.

Finally, we thank our patients and their families for letting us know what works—and what doesn't. Without their voices, this book would be without truth and soul. Their words and experiences remind us always of what we need to know next.

Introduction

HOW TO SURVIVE

YOU MAY BE A PARENT, SPOUSE, OR SIBLING—OR EVEN A LOVER, ROOM-mate, colleague, or friend. You may already know that a disorder exists or you may be aware of peculiar eating problems with someone you know, but you don't know if a serious disorder is present.

Yours is a difficult position to be in. You want to help, but you're not sure what is best. You may be witness to many behaviors that are destructive and frightening, as well as disruptive to a household or a relationship. Not knowing what to do can make you feel helpless and confused.

To add to the confusion, the guidance you receive from professionals may be completely contradictory. Some professionals tell you to get in there and take control of the eating. Others tell you that any attempt to stop the disordered eating will result in a control battle which will only make the problem worse. With no clear-cut line of approach, you may be more confused than ever.

Because you are not the one with the actual problem, however, your own difficulties may be overlooked. *Your* suffering and confusion about how to proceed may very well go unnoticed or untreated. People in your position can easily

Introduction

become the silent sufferers—the unseen victims of the eating disorder.

This book is written for you. We know how hard it is at home—and we know that you may not know what to do next. We will talk to you about how to consider the goals, given your own particular situation. We will discuss what you can do to help and what you can expect from the person with the eating disorder—and yourself.

This book is about recovery—not only that of the person with the eating disorder, but your recovery and the recovery of your relationship as well.

Since the last writing of *Surviving* (over 10 years ago), Margot and I each have traversed adolescence and young adulthood with our own children. In the last edition, we looked to our role as parents to help us speak to other parents from within the trenches. We knew both how fulfilling—and complicated— parenting could be. But we hadn't yet fully encountered what it meant to parent teenagers and young adults leaving home! A rereading of the earlier editions of *Surviving* made us realize that no manual can come close to appreciating the intricacies involved in parenting older children. Straightforward recom- mendations from the last editions miss complications and nu- ances that come with living a life with growing kids. We write this new edition informed not just with new information, but perhaps more importantly, with new life experiences.

Indeed, not only have we changed, but the culture has changed as well. As we write this edition, we are sheltered-in- place, surrounded by the fear of COVID-19 and the unknown. By the time this book is published, it is possible that the world as we know it will have significantly changed. Indeed, in the last 10 years, change in the culture evoked much change in the treatment arena. Insurance companies began to inform how treatment would evolve. Shorter-term inpatient stays became the norm and we had to creatively consider what else could allow for a higher level of care when more intensive treatment was needed. New options evolved, such as partial hospitalization programs, in-home food coaching, online call centers, peer counseling, and many new psychopharmacological medications. The question became not whether help would be needed, but rather what that help should be.

As treatment options changed, so did the role of parenting. The introduction of family-based treatment, in which parents re-feed their anorexic child, nudged parents center stage in the treatment arena. Parents have been urged to take charge of their son's or daughter's eating and weight and have been encouraged to play a more dominant role in the daily care of a child in trouble.

Questions linger however and with even more change about to occur post-COVID, more questions will come center stage. For example, for some parents, direct refeeding has allowed for full recovery of their starving son or daughter. For others, involvement (particularly when an entire family is sheltered in place) has been at best problematic, resulting in exacerbated issues of intrusion and authoritative control. What should be the carer's role in supporting the person they love and allowing their son or daughter to best take hold of their own life?

This fourth edition of *Surviving* has been written to address the changes that have occurred since the last publications of this book. Since that time, research in the field, in particular that of the Maudsley researchers (Daniel LeGrange, James Lock, Ivan Eissler, Chris Dare, George Szmukler, and others), Janet Treasure, Mary Tantillo, and Adele LaFrance, has focused on the need to attend not just to food and weight but also to the family relationships themselves.

Surviving draws on this research and takes this work one step further. In this new edition, we introduce the Relationship Model, a family and partner-oriented treatment model in which both medical stabilization and changes in family relationships are at once the focus of the work. The program establishes guidelines for involvement that interweave direct intervention with food with an understanding of how changes in relationships can help recovery. Much work and research has been done regarding what carers need to do to allow for this kind of change and how they can best set the stage for recovery. But often, even in the face of the best of treatment guidance, change remains hard. In this edition of *Surviving*, we help you pay attention to the rules and relationships you grew up with that inform how you interact today. This kind of understanding can allow for a better appreciation of why change is hard and what you can do to allow for more choice in your family and friend relationships. We have taken new information, new research—and our own life experiences—to offer you specific guidelines on how to think about how you, not just the person you love, can survive an eating disorder.

Surviving an Eating Disorder can be used as a general reference book to pick up whenever you are faced with the question "What do I do now?" However, this is not just a guidebook. *Surviving an Eating Disorder* also examines eating problems with the goal of broadening your perspective on the difficulties you see and furthering your understanding of the complex syndromes of any kind of disordered eating. The combination of perspectives and strategies offered in this book can provide you with a new and richer awareness of both the eating disorder and your relationship with the person you are concerned about.

Throughout this edition, attuned to changing perspectives regarding gender and diversity, we will be using the pronoun *they*. However, the clinical examples present specific situations and people (often female). There, we will refer to the person with regard to their identified gender. We hope that readers of all identities, races, and cultures will feel heard and attended to through our writing. The first-person stories and case examples in this book accurately reflect the feelings, experiences, and circumstances expressed by patients, their families, and friends, but all names, locales, and identifying details have been changed.

PART I

GAINING PERSPECTIVE

1.

WHAT YOU SEE

The Behavioral Aspects of Eating Disorders

I looked over at my 14-year-old daughter, Lara, as the internist spoke to us, "I'm worried that Lara's not eating" he said. "I think you'll need to speak to someone who specializes in anorexia." I looked at Lara's sticklike arms. Was she really any worse than her friends? Was this doctor on high alert for eating disorders? Maybe he didn't know what he was talking about. But watching Lara stare blankly, her face suddenly looked old to me, bony, unpleasantly pointed. My heart sank. Things had been going so well. She was a straight-A student. She never seemed like she had any problems on her mind. Had I really stopped noticing? Was something really wrong?

Barbara L., 39-year-old mother

I came home early from work with flowers, thinking I'd surprise my wife. When I put the key in the door, I was met with a frantic cry, "Wait, who is it? Ben? Don't come in yet! Wait!" I panicked. I thought the worst and raced into the apartment. And there was Nina, standing in the middle of the kitchen. A box of cake, cookies, and a pie were opened and half-eaten ice cream was melting in the container beside it. Nina looked at me angrily. "Why didn't you call?" she demanded. "Why are you home so early?" A moment before I had been so sure I would find her with another man—but this? What had I walked in on? What was happening to my wife? I remember not knowing what to do with the flowers.

Ben, 27-year-old husband

It's getting harder and harder living with Zach. It seems like he lives in the gym these days. And if he isn't in the gym, he's running— sometimes easily for two or three hours at a time. That might be great if he were training to be an athlete. But I think he's training to make sure he's out of the house. We have two young kids at home, and yes, oh by the way, a wife—me! Mostly I'm so mad at him, but lately he's been looking so sad. I'm beginning to think that something is really wrong.

Pamela, 34-year-old mother and wife

WHEN EATING HABITS BECOME EATING DISORDERS

The mother, husband, and wife in the above examples knew that something was wrong. What they were seeing was not normal behavior. In all three cases, there were clear signs that the people with whom they were involved were in trouble. Does that mean that they had an eating disorder?

When an eating disorder exists, it is recognized by certain behaviors, the most noticeable being an obsession with food, weight, and/or exercise. This obsession can take the form of binge eating, food restriction, vomiting, compulsive exercising, or other behaviors focused on eating, getting rid of, or avoiding food.

Eating disorders, however, are not merely problems with food. They are psychological disorders, many aspects of which are not apparent to an outside observer. It is often not easy to tell who is and who is not suffering with an eating disorder. Dieting, exercising, fasting, and a preoccupation with food and weight are so much a part of our culture that it is unusual to find a teenage girl or woman who is not or has not been concerned with weight. Take one look at Instagram and you will find the relentless focus on losing weight and staying healthy (the new, socially acceptable, way of saying *thin*). Health and eating regimes dominate the pages. Fashion, advertising, and entertainment idealize a female body that only one percent of women can hope to achieve. And food plans that are not necessarily healthy and are bound to fail are promoted. However, the value of thinness and health is not the only message that is communicated. Alongside the messages to be thin are ads and recipes for rich, enticing meals and desserts. Our culture seems to encourage us all to literally have our cake and eat it too.

Almost everyone is susceptible to our culture's messages. Comments like "You look so good. Did you lose weight?" perpetuate the importance of being thin. There are few people who don't enjoy these compliments. In fact, thinness is such a desirable attribute that 60 to 80 percent of college students have been on a diet within the previous year, despite most being at a healthy weight.[1]

And 97 percent of women have at least one negative thought a day related to body image.[2]

It is not just women who are being affected by the culture's messages. Men are also becoming increasingly food and weight conscious and are no longer excluded from society's emphasis on good looks, slim physique, and being in "six-pack ab" shape. In fact, men may well be at risk for "reverse anorexia," in which one sees extreme efforts to increase body size and muscle mass.[3]

And no question, when identities expand and fluidity emerges as part of one's gender experience, food and weight control have been turned to (often abusively) as ways of coping with not only identity and psychological and physiological challenges, but also bullying and discrimination. In one study, up to 42 percent of men diagnosed with an eating disorder were self-identified as homosexual or bisexual. Gay men were seven times more likely to report bingeing and 12 times more likely to report purging than heterosexual males. And in general, elevated rates of binge-eating and purging by vomiting or laxative abuse were found with people who identified as gay, lesbian, bisexual, or "mostly heterosexual" in comparison to their heterosexual peers.[4]

Once seen as a young White girl's problem, and often acknowledged to be a significant problem in the Asian American communities, we now realize that people from all ethnicities are struggling in significant ways with food and weight. For example, Black teens are 50 percent more likely than white teenagers to engage in bingeing and purging.[5] Hispanic teens have been found to suffer from bulimia more than their non-Hispanic peers.[6] And even those in the Native American community struggle, with research showing 48.1 percent of the adolescent population struggling to lose weight.[7]

Unfortunately, it is only recently that attention is being paid to the prevalence of disordered eating throughout diverse cultures. Expanded awareness and treatment options urgently need to be explored given that people of color are significantly less likely to receive help for their eating issues.

It seems that no one can escape the message that you aren't good enough the way you are.

The focus on body, dieting, and weight is particularly acute among teenagers. Teenage girls are constantly vying to be the thinnest or skipping meals to lose weight. More troubling is the fact that this dissatisfaction with one's body is occurring at even younger ages. Studies show that girls as young as three have been found to already have a preference for the culture's thin idealized body type. By age five, they can already be dieting.[8]

Regardless of the age group, it seems food and weight are on everyone's mind. Does this then mean that everyone in our society has an eating disorder? No.

An eating disorder exists when one's attitude toward food and weight has gone awry—when one's feelings about work, school, relationships, day-to-day activities, and one's experience of emotional well-being are determined by what has or has not been eaten or by a number on the scale. Most of us know what it is like to comfort or reward ourselves with food, to allow ourselves an indulgent meal after a particularly difficult day, to have the extra calories when we feel disappointed. Most of us know how it feels to wish we looked thinner in that bathing suit or to want to look particularly good for an important occasion. However, when these wishes or rewards turn into the basis of all decisions, when the pounds prevent us from going to the beach, when our looks are more important than the occasion itself, then there are indications of a problem deserving attention.

Eating problems can start in many different ways. Usually, nothing looks wrong at all at first. There is a wish to lose weight, to maintain a certain body image, to eat healthfully. Almost all of us know what that feels like. But suddenly something can go wildly and shockingly wrong.

None of us know exactly what causes an eating disorder.

How is it that someone can go through a period of intensive dieting, obsession with weight, or overeating and it won't end in a major life disruption? And yet someone else's initially same experience will land them in an endless series of residential programs in a desperate attempt to stay alive?

There are several factors involved when disordered eating becomes an eating disorder. First and likely most importantly, physiology rules. Genetically, we all are so different from one another. For example, studies show that kids who become anorexic are genetically prone to being perfectionistic, exacting, needing things in order and in place. They are the kids who need to draw inside the lines, who keep the bedroom door open exactly the same crack each night, who need to get A's when they first enter school. Imagine what happens to a kid who needs things in order when their pre-teen body starts to change, or when hormones and emotions start to fly, or even when the family is disrupted by life events, illness, or death. For these kids, change is really hard. They will hold onto anything they can to keep things the same. When everything else feels out of control, food is one thing that anyone can control. Thus it's possible that genetic proclivities are the predictors to anorexic behavior. In the more extreme situations with weight loss and starvation, research is focusing on whether there indeed is a primary physiological cause, not unlike with autism or schizophrenia.

Physiology, too, can allow for different body types, hungers, and cravings. Any woman knows that hunger increases during pre-menstrual days. What if someone has to battle that kind of increased hunger every day because of their physiological makeup? Not fair! But certainly, that can result in increased hunger, bingeing, and consequent terror at gaining weight.

Fighting one's physiological hungers may well result in binge eating and/or purging in attempts both to manage the hunger and the consequent weight gain.

And of course, our culture sets the stage for disordered eating. Not only, as described, is there a focus on being thin and fit but the culture around food and eating itself is in complete disarray. The right way to eat has replaced a focus on the right way to be. Bestselling books and Instagram influencers urge viewers and readers to give up gluten, abstain from sugar, to juice, to fast, or to give up eating completely for days at a time. The culture itself insists that people stop listening to what they feel or what they want. The intense message is that eating should be orchestrated by outside rules. This disconnection from one's body, one's needs, and one's tastes is a major contributor to the development of disordered eating.

But the thinking is that while physiology and environment can load the gun for an eating disorder, it is one's individual psychology that in many cases pulls the trigger. Food, dieting, or bingeing become ways of dealing with either the demands of one's body or the culture at large. And the problem is that, at least in the short term, the eating solutions work. Eating, restriction, or purging become ways of managing internal feelings or discomfort. For example, what may start out as real hunger turns into a binge when feelings of defeat due to the extent of the eating overwhelm physical hungers. Suddenly someone is eating to manage bad feelings about one's self—and not to manage real physiological hunger. In another instance, starving may become a way of managing someone's fear of a changing, growing adolescent body; physiologically, hungers or satiety are wiped out by a disordered need to control both food and feelings. In these cases, eating or not eating become an eating disorder because the behaviors are now satisfying psychological not physiological needs.

Consider Corey's situation for a moment. Corey is a 28-year-old who came to us for help. When Corey was a teenager and became upset due to a school event or a canceled date, she found it comforting to sit in front of the television and slowly eat a piece of chocolate cake or other dessert from her mother's well-stocked kitchen. During this time, weight was not an issue for Corey. While she always enjoyed her late-night snacks, they were certainly not the focus of her thinking or plans.

When Corey left home to go to college, however, she began to have more trying times. She felt somewhat overwhelmed by the demands of living on her own in a new environment. Frequently, she felt homesick. More and more often, she looked forward to the late-night snacks (which actually began to occur earlier and earlier in the evening). She found the food soothing and she could block out her thoughts when she ate. As the school year progressed, Corey found herself thinking about and looking forward to eating as soon as she woke up. Her thoughts started to revolve around what she would eat at mealtimes and what snacks she could buy throughout the day.

She was soon feeling that the rest of her life was secondary to eating. Consequent weight gain accelerated Corey's withdrawal from her social life to a world of food. At this point, Corey could no longer be considered a normally food-obsessed teenager; her focus on food, her social withdrawal, and the bingeing were all signs that her eating habits were now part of an eating disorder.

Karla, on the other hand, could be considered to have been eating disordered from the early age of 13. As soon as she began to develop physically, Karla recalls, the natural roundness of her shape led her to worry about becoming overweight and she started to control her food intake and weight. She decided that at five foot two it was okay to weigh 95 pounds, absolutely no more (and she found it too difficult to weigh less). Since age 13, Karla has remained 95 pounds. She is now 30 years old. She weighs herself six to ten times daily. If her weight fluctuates at all and rises above 95 pounds, she will do anything possible to make the scale show 95 again. Her efforts include exercising rigorously throughout the day and night (sometimes until three or four a.m., when her weight finally returns to 95 pounds), sitting in a sauna wrapped in plastic wrap (to sweat out the liquids), and certainly not eating or drinking anything (including water) until the scale again reaches the magical number 95. If Karla has anything planned for a day when her weight happens to be 96 pounds, she will either cancel the event or know that she will have a bad time. When asked, "How can you know you will have a bad time at a party before you get there?" Karla answers simply, "Because I'm 96 pounds and feel fat." Karla's rigid attitude certainly signals the clinical picture of an eating disorder—that is, one's experience of day-to-day situations being rigidly determined by one's weight and food intake.

THE EATING DISORDERS

When people talk about "eating disorders," they are usually referring to either anorexia nervosa, bulimia nervosa, or binge-eating disorder. But disorders around eating and weight are not always so clear-cut in description. In fact, in recent years, we most often see a picture in which many problems around food and body concerns occur at once. The diagnosis of Other

Specified Feeding or Eating Disorders (OSFED) encompasses a wide variety of ways in which trouble with food or weight can occur. For example, someone might alternate severe restriction with days of bingeing. Exercise, laxatives, and vomiting may all occur as ways to maintain a significantly low weight. Bingeing can occur when someone is half-asleep at night while rigidly healthy eating is held to during the day. There are many ways in which fear of food and weight can rule one's life.

We are also seeing more children and teens who are afraid to eat, not because they want to be thin, but because they have an aversion to certain foods or they fear feeling sick or in pain from eating (this is called ARFID or Avoidant Restrictive Food Intake Disorder). Even healthy eating can go too far. Orthorexia is characterized by an obsessive focus on healthy eating, a focus that ultimately restricts, not enhances, one's life.

At younger and younger ages, kids are now experimenting with dieting, purging, and weight loss. Kids have always been curious about drinking, smoking, and drugs. Now they are also curious about eating, restricting, diets, and changing their body shape. Experimentation with food will occur in the same way kids try to vape or take a hidden drink. Many girls (and now boys) will diet. Many will throw up or lose weight or binge. But how do we know when a problem really exists? When does experimentation with weight loss, dieting, or healthy eating turn into a problem and how do you know when to get involved?

ANOREXIA NERVOSA

Anorexia nervosa (often just referred to as anorexia) is characterized by a significant weight loss due to a purposeful attempt to stop eating. Anorexia can occur at any weight. The diagnosis doesn't have only to do with weight—it has to do with rapid weight loss and an intense fear of feeling fat. If your son or daughter is of a large body size but suddenly stops eating and loses weight quickly, this may not be a sign that they are finally getting healthy. It is possibly a sign that they are in trouble. On the other end of the spectrum, close to death at 65 pounds, someone fully in the throes of anorexia will show you where on their body they feel they need to lose weight. In an attempt to be even skinnier, calories are avoided at all costs—even if the cost is one's life. What should you look for to consider whether someone you love is in trouble?

Essential Features of Anorexia Nervosa

- Intense fear of becoming fat, which does not diminish as weight loss progresses.
- Disturbance of body image (e.g., claiming to feel fat even when emaciated).
- Quick and significant weight loss (at least 15 percent of normal body weight although, as noted, weight is not the only determinant of anorexic behavior or thinking).
- Refusal to maintain a minimal normal—or stable—body weight.
- No known physical illness that would account for the weight loss.

Mariel's diary revealed the drastic nature of her dieting. At 16, she would write a daily entry in her diary listing the food she ate each day.

This entry is typical:

10 a.m.	1 cup black coffee
	Sweet & Low
	One low fat yoghurt with berries
Noon	1 cup black coffee
	Sweet & Low
	10 carrots, 10 sticks celery
	Salad greens, tomatoes, no dressing
2 p.m.	1 vitamin A
	1 multiple vitamin
	1 vitamin B
	One health bar
7 p.m.	1 bouillon cube chicken broth and hot water
	One chicken breast or one piece of poached salmon roasted with salt and pepper
	Steamed vegetables

Mariel was 99 pounds and five foot six. That she had already passed out twice in the last month was no impediment to her harsh regime.

The attempt to lose weight usually occurs through induced starvation, but weight loss can be accelerated by vomiting, use of diuretics, or rigorous exercise. Often laxatives are tried as well in an attempt to reduce bloating or allow for immediate decrease of weight on a scale. Severe dieting or exercising can lead to alteration in the body's fat-to-muscle ratio. Changes in hormonal patterns and menstrual cycle usually (although not always) occur—sometimes even before a significant amount of weight has been lost.

Katie was 16 when her boyfriend broke up with her. Sad and confused after what she thought had been a close, year-long relationship, Katie found herself avoiding friends, binge watching shows, and binge eating food. In just four months, she gained 25 pounds. A picture of herself that she saw on Instagram resulted in panic. Almost overnight Katie decided she had to lose weight—and lose it fast. At home she would pick at her food, calculating the calories of each bite. She insisted on eating only salads, and after meals would figure out how many hours of exercise she needed to do that night to work off what she had eaten. Sometimes she'd be up for hours before she felt she had exercised enough. Within six weeks, Katie lost the weight she had gained as well as an additional 10 pounds. While Katie's weight was still not extreme, the weight loss was. Her body mass index (BMI) was not significantly low, but her behavior was signaling a problem. The refusal to eat and consequent rapid weight loss, seeing herself as overweight despite a now low weight, and her preoccupation with food and exercise were serious warning signs of anorexia nervosa. Her weight did not have to drop to 80 or 90 pounds for her to be considered eating disordered and in need of help.

How It Begins

No one starts a diet with the intention of becoming anorexic. The young woman who may ultimately find herself emaciated and near death starts out dieting like anyone else who wants to lose weight. However, for the person who becomes anorexic, the dieting and weight loss quickly take on a function that is unanticipated and unplanned. As this person begins to lose weight, they feel a newfound control in a life in which they previously did not feel effective or strong. Even if the need to starve is motivated by physiological causes, the result is a sudden feeling of power—weight is lost and everyone is telling them that they look good. Often with a touch of arrogance, they feel they have become someone who doesn't have to eat like other people do.

"When I'd be at dinner with my friends," says Margie, 17, of her months of anorexia, "I'd feel superior to everyone who was eating. I felt like I was the only one in control. The others were slaves to their hunger. It made me feel better than them."

The dieting and weight loss give meaning to one's life. Each day is a challenge—and every morning the number on the scale will say whether they have won or lost the previous day's contest. This challenge, this power, is not something that is a planned intention of the dieter but, once in effect, is hard for someone, even in the beginning stages of anorexia, to give up. Maybe a young woman was previously the "good girl," accommodating what others wanted of her. Now, perhaps for the first time, she has found a behavior that says, "You can't make me do what you want me to do. I'm not giving in to you—or to my hunger—or to my feelings. I'll eat what *I* want."

For someone who otherwise has been unassuming and shy, this is not an easy stance to abandon.

Who Is Vulnerable?

The overwhelming majority—90 percent—of people who develop anorexia are women. The age of onset is usually between 12 to 18 years, but anorexia nervosa does occur in women in their forties and fifties and we now, unfortunately, are seeing girls as young as eight and nine with anorexic behaviors. And men are certainly not immune to this disorder. While approximately 0.9 to 2.0 percent of females are diagnosed with anorexia, 0.1 to 0.3 percent of males are also at risk.[9]

As we have noted, there is as of yet no clear reason why one person becomes eating disordered and another does not. Current thinking indicates that eating disorders result from a complicated mix of biological, cultural, and psychological factors.

Susceptibility to anorexia nervosa, like susceptibility to all behaviors, is no doubt controlled in part by genetics. But at this time, little is understood about what aspects of inheritance account for anorexic behavior.

One character trait often associated with anorexia is shyness. Obviously, not all shy girls become anorexic. But in some individuals becoming obsessed with their body size may be a way of attempting to overcome feelings of incompetence, unworthiness, and ineffectiveness, thus increasing their feelings of control over their lives.

We do now know that anorexia is associated with obsessive compulsive disorder and therefore the perfectionistic strivings common to anorexics may be a biologically determined component of this disorder. We hear interesting stories about how these kids were when they were young. Often, they were the "good kid," pleasing others, highly demanding, and critical of one's self. Scratch the surface further and we often hear about the screaming, throwing furniture, slamming doors. These stories are always surprising when you're hearing them about straight-A, perfectionistic kids. But these moments speak to the difficulty, even at a young age, with change or emotions.

Of course, perfectionism and shyness do not always predict a problem with anorexia. But for someone who becomes anorexic, they are part of a bigger picture in which the perfection hides deep insecurities.

The most recent research connects the development and maintenance of anorexia with metabolic disturbances, predestined by genetic makeup.[10]

We're hoping that future work will establish physiological links that allow for better medical care of the drive toward starvation. For now, no matter the cause, the crisis of anorexia must allow for a moment for everyone to stop and better understand the person who is suffering and to consider how to best allow that person to grow, both physically and psychologically. It allows for an opportunity for change, change that perhaps has been needed long before the weight loss.

How the Disorder Progresses

While dieting may initially look normal, quickly it takes on a life of its own. There will be a preoccupation with food, dieting, and weight loss. Note that sometimes people who are *not* anorexic lose a lot of weight due to depression, physical disorders, or the syndrome of Avoidant Restrictive Food Intake Disorder (ARFID) in which fears of getting sick result in food restriction and weight loss. These problems may go undiagnosed and will result in the same type of extreme weight loss one sees in those with anorexia. The difference is that in these cases the person is not actively attempting to be thinner. Whenever extreme weight loss occurs, a doctor should be contacted to rule out causes. Only in the case of an eating disorder (other than ARFID) will you see an active attempt at weight loss.

People struggling with anorexia will ask you if they look fat. They will feel ashamed of being seen in public—because, at 90 pounds, they feel disgustingly overweight. They may be on the scale 10 times a day.

Their diets will grow more and more extreme as time goes on. Often, a normal diet becomes the start of greater and greater restriction. One or two foods will be eliminated each day. Carbs, sugar, gluten, and so on suddenly become forbidden. When anorexia starts to kick in, the person won't feel hungry (or won't admit to feeling hungry) but will be so elated to have met their restrictive food-intake goals. If they consume more than they allow, they are devastated, forlorn, filled with self-hatred "for being such a pig."

Conversations often center around food or looks. In fact, despite their own starvation, someone with anorexia often enjoys cooking, preparing meals for others, and collecting recipes. While they won't eat, their nutritional deprivation will result in constant thoughts about food. Untouched food will be hidden and stored—but never eaten. Take, for example, Mrs. Jansen, who was looking through her daughter Jada's bureau drawers for clothes to bring her after Jada left to be hospitalized for anorexia. Mrs. Jansen was surprised to find one drawer packed with high-calorie sweets. It was a shock to her that Jada could starve herself to near death and keep all that food at her fingertips.

Another particularly disturbing hallmark of anorexia nervosa is the persistent denial that anything is wrong. Hunger and fatigue are strongly denied. In fact, at a certain point, there is a genuine inability to feel hunger. Understandably, when the disorder progresses to this stage, it is extremely difficult for eating to be resumed without outside intervention. Physiological complications secondary to the anorexia are also ignored. Common medical problems can include dizziness, numbness to hands and feet, dehydration, and low blood pressure. Heart irregularities or heart or kidney failure can occur as a result of potassium depletion and severe nutritional imbalances. Loss of concentration is also common. Despite this, every person in the grips of anorexia will be (at least at first) fiercely resistant to the idea of therapy because all attempts to help or intervene are seen as a way to make them eat.

As a result of the ferocity of the denial and the tenacious hold the disorder has, the progression of anorexia nervosa can be tragic. People die. Anorexia is the most lethal psychiatric disorder, carrying a sixfold increased risk of death—four times the death risk from major depression. Studies estimate the long-term fatality rate to be over 10 percent.

Young people between the ages of 15 and 24 with anorexia have 10 times the risk of dying compared to their same-aged peers.[11]

For some people, anorexia can become a chronic problem, almost a way of life, with the sufferer never regaining a healthy weight and living a life tormented by the terror of becoming fat and driven by compulsions to exercise and eat ritualistically. For most people who have been diagnosed with anorexia, however, the disorder is an acute illness that lasts months to a few years and can be treated effectively through a combination of psychological and medical care.

BULIMIA NERVOSA

Bulimia nervosa, commonly referred to as bulimia, is usually characterized by bingeing—that is, eating large amounts of food in a short time. The binge is followed by an attempt to get rid of the food and consequent calories, in what is called the purge. In some cases, the person doesn't binge *per se* but feels compelled to get rid of anything they've eaten beyond what they had determined is okay.

You cannot tell that someone is bulimic by their weight. Someone who binges and purges is often within a normal range of weight. However, within this range, you might see jagged fluctuations. Someone may be bingeing and purging all that they eat—or restricting at other times. No matter how one is eating, a large part of what defines an eating disorder is how much time someone spends thinking about what they are going to eat. Someone who is struggling with bulimia is likely never comfortable around food. Food is the enemy and the war is endless.

Essential Features of Bulimia

- Eating a significantly large amount of food in a short amount of time and feeling that the eating is out of one's control. There is an awareness that the eating pattern is abnormal.
- Repeated attempts to lose weight through severely restrictive diets; self-induced vomiting; use of laxatives, cathartics, enemas, colonics, or diuretics; medications; or excessive exercise.
- Binge eating and purging occur on the average at least once weekly for three months.
- Fear of not being able to stop eating voluntarily.
- Depressed mood.
- Self-deprecating thoughts following eating binges.
- Self-evaluation is overly influenced by body shape and weight.

The Binge

A binge usually refers to the rapid consumption of a large amount of high-caloric food in a relatively short time. Binges can range anywhere from the intake of 1,000 to 60,000 calories or higher. However, sometimes a small amount of food (such as one piece of cake) is experienced as a binge.

"When I ate healthfully, gluten, carbs, and sugar were completely out of the question," says 24-year-old Lucy of her teenage bulimic years. "If I had *one* bite of bread, just one, I felt like I blew it! I'd stop listening to whomever was talking to me at the table. I'd start thinking, *How can I get rid of this?* I worried that my stomach would blow up and bloat. My head would be flooded with thoughts of what to do now—should I binge since I'd already blown it? Could I get rid of the food? Would anyone see? The night was blown. I was a mess."

We've met patients who go to restaurants, order a full-course meal, throw up, then go to another restaurant and eat again. Three or four full-size meals may be eaten before exhaustion hits and the person is ready to go home. And yes, it can be terribly costly. We have treated men and women whose addiction to food was so extreme that the binges cost them upwards of $100 a day. When the binges are this costly or when money is not readily available (such as in the case of a child or a teenager), stealing food can enter the picture. In the most extreme cases, we've met patients who have prostituted themselves to keep what feels like an addiction going.

Bingeing usually occurs in secret. Urges to eat are tormenting. The only relief is often strict dieting. But the consequent feelings of deprivation or the upset someone feels when even the tiniest amount of control is relinquished often begins the cycle of bingeing again. And unfortunately, when someone wants food, it's all too easy to find. One shy 18-year-old even told us that when she vacationed with her parents, she'd steal food from the half-eaten room service trays left outside of hotel rooms. Another woman, a Wall Street executive who dressed impeccably and was very well-mannered, described nightmarish evenings of rummaging for food through garbage bins in the back halls of her apartment building. She resorted to this behavior because she had ordered in food so often in the middle of the night that she could no longer stand her feelings of humiliation when met with her doorman's puzzled looks.

For some, bingeing only occurs at night when one wakes, semi-conscious from sleep, and eats—sometimes consciously—and sometimes not. The missing food in the morning may be the only way the person knows that about a rough time with food the night before.

Whenever a binge takes place, all feelings are blocked out. The food acts as an anesthetic. As one woman told us: "Once I start bingeing, it's like being in a stupor, like being drunk. Nothing else matters. Heaven help the person who tries to stop me. It's like I'm a different person. It's very humiliating—but not then, not while I'm eating. While I'm eating, *nothing* else matters."

After the Binge: Shame and Panic

Bingeing leaves everyone exhausted and uncomfortable—not just physically uncomfortable, but emotionally uncomfortable as well. Men and women tell us that they don't recognize the person they become at those times. "I hate that out-of-control, needy person," one man told us. "I feel like I become a wild animal. At those moments, I genuinely don't care what I look like, but if anyone saw me, it would look disgusting." Shame and guilt abound.

And then of course, immediately following is the terror of weight gain. The fear of what might be only one or two pounds feels overwhelming. But it's not just the weight that is feared; as frightening is the possibility that this out-of-control part of oneself will somehow be exposed.

The awful feelings of shame, panic about weight gain, and the physical discomfort inevitably lead to getting rid of the food by any means possible. That's how an endless cycle of bingeing and then purging can begin.

The Purge

Purging can take different forms. Most often it involves vomiting or laxative abuse. Other forms of purging include the use of diuretics, enemas, colonics, fasting, strict dieting, rigorous exercising, diet pills, and/or the abuse of amphetamine, cocaine, or Adderall (these latter to suppress hunger on days following a binge).

The amount of purging varies from person to person. Some people binge and vomit a few times a month, others over twenty times a day. Sometimes the vomiting is induced in the middle of a binge so the eating can continue. Other times, vomiting is turned to only after all the food has been consumed. Vomiting as a solution begins benignly, almost by accident, and only gradually becomes a ritualistic part of the bulimic cycle. In many ways, purging starts out as a magical solution to the binge. But the magic comes at a huge cost.

Laxatives can be used as a way of purging as well, often not just to lose weight but also to get rid of the feeling that one's stomach is full. No one starts with more than one or two laxatives at a time but the irony about laxative abuse is that by the time the laxatives work, the food has already been digested and the calories absorbed. Thus, laxative use gives the illusion of weight loss (since water weight is lost and stomachs do flatten), but in actuality, calories are still retained and weight is put on. Enemas, diuretics, and colonics are also used like laxatives to eliminate a feeling of fullness by facilitating or speeding up the body's usual function of voiding. Like laxatives, they, too, momentarily eliminate water, but calories remain ingested.

In some cases, the terror of gaining weight results in a compulsion to chew and spit out food. If one bite of food is actually swallowed, panic ensues. Huge quantities of food can be tasted this way, but nothing is actually ingested. Of course, if little food is eaten at other times during the day, this torturous behavior can lead to anorexic weight loss despite the ongoing presence of food in the picture.

Other forms of purging (diet pills, drug use, fasting, and/ or rigorous exercise) are used to inhibit eating or to burn off the calories after a binge. One of the more dangerous forms of purging occurs with some sufferers of type 1 diabetes. Here, insulin is purposely restricted in an attempt to increase blood sugar level and consequently lose weight. This type of purging, colloquially called "diabulimia" can lead to severe medical destabilization and, in the worst cases, death.

Usually, however, the consequences of bulimia are more psychological than they are physical.

John, 34, had a pattern of bingeing continuously for a week or two following a disappointment or frustration in his life. During these times, he ate throughout the day, missed work, stopped shaving and caring for himself, and could easily put on 20 pounds. At a certain point of exhaustion or self-disgust (it was never clear to him when this would occur), he would stop bingeing and begin to eat healthfully, but he would also begin exercising in what was almost a panic-stricken manner. One hour of swimming preceded 10 miles of fast-paced jogging. A strenuous workout ritual was what he had to look forward to when he returned home from work. If John was lax in any of these regimens, he became severely self-critical, anxious, and was plagued with thoughts of gaining weight. John's exercise regimen was as drastic a purge as vomiting was for others previously mentioned.

How It Begins—"It Won't Happen to Me"

No one who decides to control weight by vomiting, laxative use, or any other forms of purging ever believes that they will end up in an out-of-control cycle of bingeing and purging. In fact, bulimia always starts out as a way of being *in* control—in control of food, of weight, of one's size, of one's image.

"I didn't think it was really such a bad thing," said Rachel, 38 and bulimic for 20 years. "When I first started purging, I'd throw up about once or twice a month. I figured other people smoked, or drank, or did drugs. I didn't do any of those things; so I figured they all had their thing, this was mine."

But what happened to Rachel was fairly typical. Knowing she could vomit provided the excuse to give in to the urge to eat more and more often, until she was caught up in a desperate cycle of bingeing and purging that reached its current twice-daily frequency.

No matter the method, purging provides the momentary perfect solution.

"So what?" we hear again and again. "I feel so relieved at the moment. What's so bad about throwing up or using laxatives. Isn't it better than feeling fat?"

This is such a sad statement about the extreme pressure to be thin in our culture. The truth is that there is a lot that is "so bad" about purging.

The main problem with these behaviors is that they stop being only about food and weight. They become a way to control one's feelings, one's identity, even one's relationships. The constant obsession with food and weight become as torturous as the eating and purging itself. Once this cycle is started, it is completely unclear who will actually ever be able to stop. Not one person starts this with the idea that they will be stuck thinking about it every day of their life.

Louisa, 18, talked tearfully of trying to get through the days at college struggling with bulimia:

> *Every day I wake up and say I'm going to be "good" today. Usually I make it until dinner without bingeing or getting sick, but the evenings are always the worst. Sometimes I actually make it to bed—but then I lie there not being able to sleep. I keep thinking if I just ate a little it would put me to sleep. Sometimes I'll toss and turn till three or four a.m., but I always end up giving in and eating my roommate's food or even going out to the food court at school. Even if I only eat one thing, like a muffin or one candy bar, I have to throw it up or it will sit in my stomach and I can't sleep. What kills me is that every day for*

*three years I've been doing this—starting out "good" and
then blowing it every night. I feel like something crazy is
happening to me. Am I going to spend the rest of my life
fighting with this thing?*

Others describe putting cleaning powder on food that they
don't want to eat, dumping food in the garbage, having parents
or roommates hide or lock up food. This is always to no avail.
Food is washed, dug up from under the trash, or found no
matter where the hiding place is. The struggle not to binge is as
profound as the struggle for any addict trying to kick a habit.

Medical complications are often minimal, though they can
include fatigue, sore throats, ulcerated esophagi, tooth decay, and,
worse, heart disturbances due to potassium depletion. Laxative
abuse, in particular, can lead to constipation, gastrointestinal
bleeding, rectal prolapse, and a physiological dependence on
the laxatives in order to void. But even when someone is aware
of these complications, they are not motivators to change. Instead, these problems are seen as proof of being a terrible person. "Look at what I'm doing to myself" we frequently hear.
"I'm slowly killing myself and I won't even stop."

Complications that lead to death are less common in bulimia, but if treatment is not pursued, bulimia can become a
lifelong progressive disorder in which more and more of the
person's daily activities and thoughts are oriented around food.

Who Is Vulnerable?

Bulimia usually starts in adolescence or young adulthood, although recently the age of onset is occurring in kids as young
as 9 or 10 and in people well into their forties and fifties.

As with the other eating disorders, bulimia develops as a result of complex bio-psycho-social factors. Research indicates that physiological components may play a role in cravings and the need to purge. Additionally, the culture helps foster problematic beliefs regarding weight and body image. If someone feels insecure about one's self in any arena, it's very easy to turn that anxiety onto one's body. Someone who turns to bulimia may be at a stressful point in their life (yes, even 10-year-olds feel stress). Often there is a focus on the outside world—friends, parents, lovers—to tell someone whether they are good enough. Others' judgment, not one's own, is relied upon to determine one's worthiness. And if someone is turning to the outside world to tell them if they are okay, it only takes minutes on the internet to learn that the outside world thinks you should be thin. Vulnerable to what others think, it is easy to turn to one's body and wonder, "Am I good enough?" For the majority of people in normal bodies, the culture's messages will say *NO*.

When someone doesn't have a confident sense of self, often they are conforming and eager to please, hiding anger, upset, or other negative feelings from themselves and others. In the safety of one's home, someone may indeed look angry, even at times tyrannical! But it may remain unclear what is really of concern. Food then becomes an outlet for all the feelings and conflicts that cannot be exposed or perhaps even known. Running to one's room and slamming the door because homework has to be done, for example, may cover the more raw feelings of not having been chosen for the soccer team. Bingeing and purging can serve to block or let out feelings that are experienced as unacceptable.

Approximately 1.5 percent of women and 0.5 percent of men will turn to bulimia during their lives.[12]

At least 90 percent of those who struggle with bulimia are women. However, it is possible that there are more men who are bulimic but, since they are less likely to seek treatment, there are no reliable statistics on them. One reason for this is the shame experienced by men who binge and vomit because bulimia is still, for the most part, considered a women's disease.

Many people who exercise to offset binges may deny they have a problem. Sometimes the exercise alone (separate from actual bingeing) may be a way to deal with problems that don't actually have to do with fitness or strength. For example, excessive body building (especially but not only with the use of steroids) can be a sign that the focus on the body is not only an attempt at improving fitness. Instead, ever increasing strength and fitness may be a means of compensating for poor self-esteem or other emotional concerns. When exercise interferes with relationships or life, it certainly is a question as to whether a disorder is in the making. Also, when rigorous exercise compensates for weight gain from bingeing, the cycle of overeating and exercising may well be a way of dealing with stress and the possibility of an eating disorder needs to be questioned. However, given that exercising in and of itself is not usually worrisome (whereas vomiting is), exercisers can go years without anyone noticing that a problem has developed.

BINGE-EATING DISORDER

Binge-eating disorder is characterized by uncontrollable eating followed by feelings of guilt and shame. The eating may start out as pleasurable, but quickly feels out of control and is experienced as abnormal. Someone who likes snacks, lives on carbohydrates and soft drinks, and can't resist desserts is not necessarily a binge eater. However, if food is hoarded in one's room or car, if someone urgently stuffs oneself when no one is looking, if food is no longer enjoyed but obsessively craved—then a problem may indeed exist. In these situations, the person definitely knows that something is wrong.

Binge eating without purging inevitably results in weight gain. Yet not everyone who is in a large body has an eating disorder. We are frequently asked by parents who notice their child's weight gain if this gain is the result of their son or daughter having an eating disorder. It is very important not to panic regarding your child's weight fluctuations. Weight gain does not necessarily mean that there is a problem to deal with! For example, preteens often gain weight as their body prepares for adolescent growth changes. A parent's anxiety over normal or temporary bodily changes can set the stage for a lifetime of a body pre-occupation, a lifetime of someone believing that they are not okay. No question, for many, this can set the stage for a lifetime of disordered eating in which a normal body is again and again attempted to be "fixed."

Infant weight charts are often a healthy indicator of size and growth patterns over childhood and teenage years. A consistently large baby is more than likely going to grow to become a large child. A problem should be defined when someone jumps off the normal trajectory of their childhood weight chart in a sudden or jagged way or when there are visible signs of binge eating.

Binge-eating disorder is often confused with obesity. Obesity is a term used when someone weighs more than 25 percent above their expected normal body weight (or when their BMI is greater than 30). According to some estimates, half of all Americans are overweight and a quarter are obese. Weight gain can result from a poor diet, lack of exercise, or genetic factors. There is so much shame involved in admitting that one binges, however, that few people report symptoms of binge-eating disorder. Of importance, in and of itself, binge-eating disorder is not defined by weight. It is a psychological disorder defined by one's use of food to cope with stress, emotional distress, and daily problems. And of importance, binge-eating disorder can easily result from a push to be smaller than one's normal and predictable weight. It is critical to know that dieting can very well lead to this kind of serious eating disorder.

Dieting almost always creates a sense of deprivation. For many, the feeling of deprivation eventually gives way to a break in the diet and forbidden foods are urgently turned to. The despair over blowing it results in more bingeing—or a return to a restrictive diet—which yet again sets up a cycle of yo-yo dieting. While dieting is almost always mistakenly seen as the solution, it is not the answer. Almost 95 percent of diets fail, resulting in a return to bingeing—and often even more weight gain.

Physiologically, there are reasons why dieting is so problematic. When food is restricted, the body goes into starvation mode. All bodily systems quiet down so that less energy is used and thus fewer calories are needed. Even the stomach stops churning as quickly as usual. This means that when more food is eaten again, metabolism is slower and calories are not rapidly burned so, quickly, weight will be gained. Also, diets provoke the brain to go into an intense mode of looking for food to save the body. Thus, when food is available (at a party, office meeting, or just at a normal meal) intense physiological cravings can set in and it can be harder than usual to say no. The reality is that with most diets, ultimately lost weight (and sometimes even more than has been lost) is regained.

As with the other eating disorders, the work with binge eating is both to develop sustainable, unrestrictive ways of eating that allow more of a focus on what one needs, with regard to both physical and psychological hungers.

Essential Features of Binge-Eating Disorder

- Binge eating accompanied by an awareness that the eating pattern is abnormal.
- Fear of not being able to stop eating voluntarily.
- Bingeing occurs, on average, once a week for at least three months.
- Depressed mood.
- Self-deprecating thoughts following the binges.

How It Starts

Unlike anorexia and bulimia, binge eating generally has a more gradual beginning. It often starts in early childhood when eating patterns are formed. Sometimes food is used early on as a retreat from feelings, as a way to feel good, or as an activity to fill otherwise empty time or empty feelings. Eating patterns that do not create weight gain for the growing child can result in weight problems when the person stops growing. When binge eating starts in young adulthood, it is often at times of stress when the person feels ill-equipped to handle certain frustrations and emotions.

But, as noted, binge eating can also be the result of well-intentioned attempts to make one's body smaller than what it should be. Putting a child on a diet may be the most predictable way to ensure that binge eating will secretively and enduringly occur.

Who Is Vulnerable?

Binge eating, like bulimia and anorexia nervosa, is a complicated disorder with psychological, physiological, and cultural factors contributing to its development.

We now know that cravings can be physiologically derived, with serotonin depletion accounting for some of these urges. In these cases, the cravings may be more extreme than they are for others. Here, food acts as a drug to help calm what otherwise feels to be an out-of-control sense of urgent need.

Lizzie, 25, told us, "My girlfriends tell me that they get really hungry and crave food right before their period. But I feel that all the time. It's just not fair."

Constantly surrounded by the availability of rich, super-sized portions of food, yet also surrounded by images of model-sized influencers, Lizzie, like so many others, tried to make her way with an ever-changing array of diets. Being of a larger body size since she was born, and likely having physiological hungers that she felt she had to suppress, Lizzie led a life of self-reproach, body hatred, and ongoing ever-thwarted attempts to change who she was. Lizzie's bingeing was a result of physiology and culture, terribly combined. And, too, the eating then became a way of dealing with the ongoing feelings of defeat, as well as a growing number of other stressors. The psychological soothing aspect of bingeing soon was as important a developmental factor as anything else.

Unlike with anorexia and bulimia, a relatively high proportion of men struggle with binge eating. In fact, 3.5 of women and 2.0 percent of men report having had binge-eating disorder during their life.[13]

However, given the still-tilted cultural preference for women to be small and the acceptance of men being large, treatment is sought much more frequently by women than men. Family genetics and dynamics can also allow for the development of binge-eating disorders. Any family with genetics resulting in larger body types will struggle with the culture's thin values, potentially setting up the binge-diet cycling that was just described.

Anna Lee, 14 years old, having gained a significant amount of weight throughout middle school, was sent to us by her desperate parents. She had already failed at her third diet plan. She told us:

> *In my family, at every meal my parents talked about what was healthy, what wasn't. If I wanted a second helping of something, I would be told that I was eating too much, that I could get fat. Treats and desserts were only allowed on special occasions. I learned pretty quickly that it was bad to want more. You can imagine how wildly I ended up indulging when I was at my friend's house where they could eat anything they wanted.*

How the Disorder Progresses—When Feelings Make It Worse

If someone is turning to food to cope or to offset feelings of deprivation, binge eating can often be extremely difficult to stop.

"I kicked alcohol and cocaine," one man told us, "but food—it's always around and you have to eat. It's been harder for me to stop bingeing on food than it was to stop anything else."

Binge eating indeed can block out feelings or calm someone down—but at a terribly high price. The psychological torment

involved in this disorder, combined with the poor health results of yo-yo dieting, can result in a life of despair and never
feeling good enough. What gets lost is understanding the role
food has played in ways that have nothing to do with food. It is
one thing if someone is eating because they are hungry—or just
enjoying food. It is another thing when people eat because they
feel they are hopeless about the way they look and the eating is
a way of giving up. If this is the case or if food has repetitively
become a way of soothing one's self or expressing inner feelings,
then the emotional reasons for bingeing need to be questioned.

Binge eating has only recently been taken seriously as a
problem in and of itself. Usually, weight was seen as the problem and people struggling were sent to strict weight-loss programs, where the focus was primarily on limiting food intake
and exercise. Only recently have programs developed to address binge eating as a serious problem in and of itself with the
same kind of psychological concerns that prevail in anorexia
or bulimia.

Sharon, a 24-year-old, shared her distraught feelings with us:

> I keep going to different eating-disorder groups and facil-
> ities, and it's clear I don't belong there. I don't throw up,
> I'm not too thin, I'm not a perfectionist about my size and
> looks. Then, when I try going to a diet group like Weight
> Watchers it's clear I don't belong there either. It's not sim-
> ply a matter of dieting for me. I know how to diet. I don't
> know how to stop the binges. It seems wherever I go I have
> the wrong problem. I can't even get this right.

Without the obviously strange and damaging behavior of
vomiting, bingeing is less likely to be identified as a serious

problem. It often is misperceived as a stubborn lack of self-control. This mislabeling of the problem can keep the cycle going for years. Only when a sustainable way of eating and taking care of oneself is established and when someone can question what besides food one is hungry for, is there the possibility of change.

ORTHOREXIA

Eating healthfully has become almost a new religion not only in Western cultures, but all over the world. What's wrong with that?

In and of itself, paying attention to what allows for good health is of course a good idea. But in our data-driven world, ever-new research tells us what to eat and what not to eat in order to be healthy. The research is often wrong—and it leaves out a huge part of what it means to be healthy, which is to listen to one's hungers and to better know what your own body needs at different times.

There is so much new advice as to what to eat and what not to eat, it's not worth our listing here. What concerns us is that with every new food plan, fasting regime, and dietary restrictions, what is lost is self-awareness, attention to hunger cues, and an internal sense of what feels healthy and what doesn't.

No question we all should pay attention to research. Sugar, fructose, and chemically laden products as regular parts of an ongoing diet are just not good for our bodies. That said, neither for the most part, are alcoholic drinks. Does that mean one should never drink? Of course not. There are times to relax and times to celebrate, when a drink can be a part of the experience. So it is true with food—of any type!

Essential Features of Orthorexia

Healthy eating becomes an orthorexic eating disorder when preoccupation with eating begins to interfere with one's life—or one's health. Introduced as a disorder in 1997, Dr. Steven Bratman noted that dietary restrictions intended to promote health actually were leading to unhealthy lives, riddled by anxiety and sometimes, social isolation. Orthorexia means that someone is no longer listening to one's self but is using outside rules and restrictions to regulate not only food but also emotions and a sense of one's identity as well.

Who Is at Risk?

Similar to other eating disorders, orthorexia is not merely a problem having to do with food or weight. Over time, an attempt at healthy eating can take on an almost maniacal and psychological momentum, in which food itself begins to define how someone feels about one's self. Interestingly, research indicates that men may be more likely to suffer from orthorexia than women.

Athletes in particular can start out with a food plan that initially allows for health and strength. But when that plan devolves into a means of self-definition, when eating interferes with one's day-to-day life (i.e., social situations or meals avoided, days planned around food intake, feelings of fear or despair if something unhealthy is eaten), then healthy eating has devolved into an eating disorder. Orthorexia is on the rise, with research showing prevalence rates of 6.9 percent, more that anorexia and bulimia combined.[14]

How Orthorexia Evolves

Healthy eating always starts out as just that—an attempt to feel healthier, stronger, thinner, or fitter. But a problem develops when this becomes an obsession to eat certain foods. In such cases, moderation in eating is lost and, ultimately, what one eats, instead of inner feelings or values, starts to define one's sense of self. Much time is spent thinking about food and planning what will be eaten. Interestingly, this focus can reduce anxiety and can redirect someone from worrying about relationships, emotions, or any feeling of helplessness in general. Certainly food is easier to control than relationships or feelings! But when a problem exists, eating behaviors become the main way to negotiate both internal and external difficulties, leaving the person with much less possibility of dealing with or changing the real problems at hand.

Rachel, 15 years old, came to us because her diet had become so restricted that she had begun to cut out all food groups except vegetables and greens. With a consequent weight drop, her parents worried and insisted she speak to someone. Rachel sat in my office crying. "I really was okay with the way I looked" she told me. "I try to be a good person in so many ways. But before I started to pay attention, what I ate was so unhealthy—chips and hamburgers and a lot of ice cream. But when I tried to be good with food, every book and Instagram notice had a different idea about what was good—I had to avoid flour, then sugar, then animal products. I genuinely don't know what it means to be *good* anymore. No matter what I eat, it's wrong."

At 15, Rachel understandably was trying to figure out who she was, how she should be. She wanted to eat in the best way possible. But just because food that is consumed is nutritious, it doesn't mean that the way it is consumed is healthy. When food becomes a way of defining one's identity, when flexibility—and fun—with food is taken out of the mix, certainly a potential problem needs to be explored.

Here are some things to look for when questioning whether healthy eating has gotten out of control:

- Compulsive checking of ingredient lists and nutritional labels and an increase in concern about the health of ingredients.
- Cutting out an increasing number of food groups (all sugar, all carbs, all dairy, all meat, all animal products) so that all that is eaten is considered healthy or clean.
- Spending hours per day thinking about what food might be served at upcoming events.
- Obsessive following of food and "healthy lifestyle" blogs on social media sites.
- Body image concerns may or may not be present.

AVOIDANT RESTRICTIVE FOOD INTAKE DISORDER (ARFID)

Recently we have seen more and more kids and young adults who don't fit the usual eating-disorder picture. While there are clear signs of food restriction and weight loss, there is not a focus on weight or looks. This disorder, Avoidant Restrictive Food Intake Disorder (ARFID), can result in medical instability due to weight loss but also has a tremendous psychological toll with regard to the intense fear that starts to surround eating. Fear of stomach pain and vomiting often result in extreme picky eating and food restriction.

Essential Features Involve

- Apparent lack of interest in food.
- Food avoidance due to texture and smells that over time results in a limited range of preferred food.
- Fear that eating will cause stomach pains, choking, or vomiting.
- Dramatic weight loss.
- Constipation, cold intolerance, lethargy, or excess energy.
- No concern about body image or weight.
- Medical signs of abnormalities (anemia, low thyroid and hormone levels, low potassium, low blood cell counts, slow heart rate).

How It Begins

ARFID is only newly understood. It can start as a result of a bad experience with food (i.e., a stomach virus that associates food with vomiting) or as a result of childhood textural sensitivities. Sometimes a picky eater can develop food avoidance if too much focus is put on food. One of the few ways that kids have control is in the realm of eating. Sometimes the restriction feels like the only way to be in control of one's life. This is maddening to parents who find that they can't make their child eat. The restriction becomes oddly empowering (maybe even unwittingly so) to the son or daughter who decides what will or will not go in their body. But what may start out as the win of a control battle suddenly has a life of its own and fears about eating take over. Problems in school, work, or the social arena can develop due to difficulties eating with others or the need for extended time to eat anything.

Who Is Vulnerable?

As with all eating disorders, the risk factors for ARFID involve a range of biological, psychological, and sociocultural issues. These factors may interact differently in different people, which means two people with the same eating disorder can have very diverse perspectives, experiences, and symptoms. While AR-FID is sometimes seen as part of the picture when someone is autistic, intellectually disabled, or has attention deficits, there are many other reasons for food restriction to develop. Often ARFID is a result of anxiety. Kids who are anxious at a young age will likely be anxious about what they eat, even if food isn't the main cause of their concerns. Being able to control food intake becomes a calming but thwarted way of controlling anxiety in general. Over time, in an attempt to feel in control in at least one area of their lives, food restriction grows increasingly worse.

That said, it is important to know that picky eating is *not* an eating disorder. Just because your child doesn't eat everything that is served or prefers sweets to vegetables does not mean that a problem is at hand. In fact, pushing kids to eat more than they want, as long as they are medically stable, may result in intense control battles and the possibility that ARFID could develop as the child's only way of feeling agency in one's own life. Kids go through many stages of avoiding certain foods, preferring others. In and of itself, this is not reason to be concerned.

We know of one young man who, when he was a kid, would only eat pancakes, chicken nuggets, pasta, and cold cereal. When his family traveled, they would literally take with them a suitcase of cereal and nuggets. Otherwise, their son wouldn't be interested in food at all. But their doctor told the parents that enough nutrition is infused in cold cereals and this boy's parents needed to avoid food battles. And while their son teetered on the edge of the lowest end of weight charts, he tended to be a healthy kid. Interestingly enough, by the time their son was a teen, he was eating steak and vegetables, was six foot two, and was incredibly healthy. "What changed?" we asked him. "I got bored of what I was eating" was the reply.

So don't be afraid if your child is a picky eater. As long as they are medically healthy, assume that peer pressure—and boredom—may well allow for change over time.

However there are times to be concerned. If medical illnesses ensue or if there is a drop in the normal trajectory of a child's weight or growth chart, do pay attention. If food refusal is accompanied by anxiety, social isolation, or change in moods, a more serious problem may indeed be developing. In any of these cases, don't go it alone. Both a medical and psychological evaluation should be pursued to assess what help may be needed next.

WHAT YOU CAN OBSERVE—AND WHAT YOU CAN'T

This chapter has focused on the observable aspects of eating disorders. Many people do not fit neatly into one category or the other. Some people exhibit traits from more than one category. Other people may change their behavior over time; so, for example, they start out with symptoms that typify anorexia and move into behaviors that are more characteristic of bulimia. Remember, the most common diagnosis at the time of writing this book is Other Specified Feeding or Eating Disorders (OSFED), meaning that someone may exhibit several kinds of disordered eating, purging, or restrictions at once.

In many situations serious eating problems go on far too long without notice. The following checklists will help you identify a situation that deserves your attention. The importance of educating yourself and having a clearer picture of what you are observing is not to categorize the person, but rather to have the information you will need to deal effectively with the situation.

The lists below describe signs of disordered eating that may be visible to the outside observer. These lists are not all-inclusive of every symptom, but instead focus on what you can observe. Pay attention to what you see. In some cases, the problem will be strikingly clear. In others, this information can be used to help a professional make a diagnostic determination. Remember though that some of the most critical characteristics of an eating disorder are those you won't be able to see—the unspoken sadness, confusion, and fears, the relentless obsession with what and when someone can eat. Those more complicated signs will be addressed in the chapters to follow.

WARNING SIGNS AND SYMPTOMS OF ANOREXIA NERVOSA

____Rapid weight loss (no matter what the actual weight).

____Signs of restricted eating (unusually low intake of food), such as severe diets or fasting.

____Odd food rituals, such as counting bites of food, cutting food into tiny pieces, or preparing food for others while refusing to eat.

____Intense fear of feeling or becoming fat, regardless of low weight.

____Fear of food and situations where food may be present.

____Rigid exercise regimes.

____Dressing in layers to hide weight loss.

____Bingeing.

____Use of laxatives, enemas, or diuretics to get rid of food.

____Frequent weighing.

____Cessation of menstruation without physiological cause.

____Dizziness and fainting spells.

____Mood shifts.

____Feelings of self-worth are determined by what is or is not eaten.

____Withdrawal from people.

WARNING SIGNS AND SYMPTOMS OF BULIMIA NERVOSA

____Bingeing.

____Secretive eating, evidenced by missing food.

____Preoccupation with and constant talk about food and/ or weight.

____Self-disparagement when too much has been eaten.

____Bathroom visits after meals.

____Signs of vomiting, laxative abuse, or fasting.

____The use of diet pills.

____Rigid and harsh exercise regimes.

____Fear of being fat, regardless of weight.

____Swollen glands, puffiness in the cheeks, or broken blood vessels under the eyes.

____Unexplained tooth decay.

____Frequent weight fluctuations, often within a 10-to-15-pound range.

____Mood shifts that include depression, sadness, guilt, and self-hate.

____Severe self-criticism.

____Ongoing need for approval regarding looks and weight.

____Self-worth determined by weight.

WARNING SIGNS AND SYMPTOMS OF BINGE-EATING DISORDER

____Bingeing or frequent grabbing of food.

____Eating little in public while maintaining a high weight.

____ Secretive eating and hording of food.

____Feelings about self are based on weight and control of eating.

____Feeling tormented by eating habits.

____Weight is the focus of life.

WARNING SIGNS AND SYMPTOMS OF ORTHOREXIA

____Compulsive checking of ingredient lists and nutritional labels.

____Increase in concern about the health of ingredients.

____Cutting out an increasing number of food groups (all sugar, all carbs, all dairy, all meat, all animal products).

____An inability to eat anything but a narrow group of foods that are deemed healthy or pure.

____Unusual interest in the health of what others are eating.

____Signs of distress when "safe" or "healthy" foods aren't available.

____Obsessive following of food and "healthy lifestyle" blogs on social media.

____Body image concerns may or may not be present.

WARNING SIGNS AND SYMPTOMS OF AVOIDANT RESTRICTIVE FOOD INTAKE DISORDER

___Dramatic weight loss.

___Reports of constipation, abdominal pain, cold intolerance, lethargy, and/or excess energy.

___Reports of consistent, vague gastrointestinal issues (upset stomach, feels full, vomiting, etc.) around mealtimes that have no known cause.

___Dramatic restriction in types, textures, or amount of food eaten.

___Fears of choking or vomiting.

___Lack of appetite or interest in food.

___No body image disturbance or fear of weight gain.

2.

HIDDEN FEELINGS

The Psychological Aspects of Eating Disorders

WHEN 23-YEAR-OLD JOYCE CAME IN FOR A TREATMENT CONSULTA-tion for bulimia, she explained her situation this way: "I have a nice apartment, a good job, a terrific boyfriend. Everything would be going okay if it weren't for the bingeing and vomiting. I've tried to make myself stop but I can't. If you could just help me get rid of the bulimia, I'd be okay. I'm worried it's going to ruin my health."

Joyce was upset and confused by her eating disorder. Why was she bingeing even though it was so offensive to her? Was she just lacking willpower? When they learned of Joyce's eating disorder, her parents were also confused. Joyce seemed to have everything going for her. What was wrong? Joyce herself didn't know. All she knew was that she couldn't stop bingeing and didn't want to be fat. For Joyce, the reasons she was compelled to binge and vomit were as unknown to her as they were to those observing her.

WHAT'S GOING ON INSIDE?

There's no question that physiological and genetic factors certainly create the base for the development of many eating disorders. Research, for example, has now implicated faulty metabolic processes as well as genetic composition in the emergence and reoccurrence of anorexia.[1] And certainly much has been written about regarding the physiological basis of food cravings.

But while no doubt genetic factors may set the stage for disordered eating and weight fluctuations, eating disorders are not merely problems with food or weight. When any eating disorder emerges, it is an opportunity to understand how food intake and weight control may be used to solve unseen emotional conflicts or difficulties that in fact have little to do with either food or weight. While stabilizing health is always the first priority, a focus only on healthier eating habits or stronger willpower will not make the problems disappear.

No matter what the disorder, when a crisis arises of any sort, it is an opportunity to pay attention. And when someone is in the throes of an eating disorder, it is indeed a crisis. That means, it is a time to listen and to question what else may be wrong. If nothing else, we certainly see normal family patterns severely disrupted when someone stops eating or is bingeing, purging, or intensely focused on food. We want this book to be an invitation, an opportunity of sorts, to allow a crisis to be a time of questioning. What is working in your family? What is working with your friend, spouse, or loved one? And what isn't? There may be a genetic base to why your son or daughter is anorexic, but the disorder itself may have taken on a meaning of its own for this person. Understanding what eating or not eating means to someone can often allow more possibilities of what is needed for recovery.

Jill, 25 years old, in recovery from anorexia, describes her experience:

> When I was starving myself, all I felt was that I had to. There was no rhyme or reason to it. You could not have convinced me it had anything to do with something emotional or psychological. It took time for me to see how frightened I was and how I had to feel in absolute control. I always felt that feelings got in the way of my life. I had no idea that focusing on being thin had anything to do with making sure I wouldn't feel anything. It seems strange now, even a little pathetic, but not eating was really a way to make sure I didn't feel anything. I was the girl who never cried. Only now am I beginning to see that crying isn't such a bad thing. I miss how powerful I felt when I was the thinnest in the room but I'm beginning to see how much else I missed when all I thought about was food.

IS SHE TRYING TO HURT HERSELF?

"But it's so destructive. Is she trying to hurt herself?" Joyce's mother wanted to know. The question is a common one. Eating disorders are destructive. They take a great toll, emotionally and physically. But this is not by design. Only when you understand the ways in which an eating disorder is someone's attempt to deal with feelings or to feel better about one's self can you see that the destructiveness is a by-product of the problem, not an intent. In fact, the self-destructiveness of binge eating and bulimia causes the individual great anguish and is often a motivator to stop.

"Tell me *again* about the side effects and risks of death," requested a young woman who was trying to stop daily bingeing and vomiting. "Maybe if I can really focus on how I am hurting myself, I can finally stop."

In anorexia, the destructiveness is flatly denied. Even on the brink of death, someone struggling with anorexia sees their starving as essential to their sense of competence and strength. It feels necessary to life, even as it kills.

In every eating disorder, it is only when the person is able to find healthier means of taking care of one's self and generating internal sources of self-esteem that they can give up the attempts at coping that have, ironically and tragically, led to further emotional and physical damage. Only by understanding the protective and adaptive functions of these behaviors can *you* begin to appreciate why it may be so hard for someone to just give it up.

AN EATING DISORDER IS AN EXTERNAL SOLUTION TO INNER TURMOIL

A focus on body size can actually be much more than a worry about appearance. It can also be a way to convert a worry about something inside to something outside. For example, if the concern "Am I good enough?" becomes "Am I thin enough?" the scale becomes an external way of trying to measure something that otherwise may be impossible to directly assess.

In a now quite famous study, researcher Catherine Steiner-Adair evaluated preteens to consider which young girls were most vulnerable to developing disordered eating. The girls were first asked what they thought women were supposed to be in our culture. "We're supposed to get married, have kids, have a profession, be beautiful . . ." they answered. Then they were asked what goals they had for themselves. The girls divided into two general groups. Some girls—despite the likely impossibility of the goals—said that they essentially wanted it all—to be beautiful, to be a mother, to be successful—essentially to be a superwoman. Others seemed more discerning—they would get a career, have kids later. Or maybe they would focus on having a family—what they really wanted more than anything was to be a mom. The girls were then given eating disorder questionnaires. Interestingly, the girls who wanted to be superwomen showed significant signs of becoming eating disordered. The girls who had more of a sense of themselves, who focused more on what they personally wanted instead of what the culture wanted, clearly were less troubled about their bodies and food.[2]

The implication of this study is that for girls who become eating disordered, there is a lack of confidence regarding one's own feelings, values, and self-worth. They turn to the outside world—be it the culture's values, their partners' wishes, the scale, their parents—to determine how—and whom—they should be.

No question the culture is changing. Boys now are diagnosed with bulimia and girls are learning to speak up. But when someone finds themselves paying attention to others' needs more than their own, feelings, wishes, and needs can be kept private and secret—sometimes even secret from one's self. Angry, aggressive feelings are seen as bad and unacceptable rather than the basis of healthy assertion. What then happens to those feelings?

Someone who becomes eating disordered has often taken these messages to an extreme. They are the quiet, unseen kid who has learned not to show what is bothering them. They hide their emotions, even as the disorder progresses. They learn to feel good about themselves through pleasing others, while their own "appetites" are suppressed—or not even known.

A year or two into treatment, Rose began to discover that when she binged and threw up, it was more about feeling secure than about food:

> It started to dawn on me that the bingeing and purging weren't entirely about my weight—and then I noticed a certain pattern. When I was with a man, I was not bingeing. If someone was sleeping in my bed at night there was no urge to binge. It wasn't just that I couldn't binge because someone was there, but that the urge was gone! I noticed this when I started keeping a journal of my feelings and experiences. If a man likes me, I feel pretty and confident. If no one is there, I feel awful about myself—as if I am two different people. It's bizarre to me that a stranger can completely change the way I feel about myself.

ANXIETY

As strange as it may initially sound, anxiety can be a very useful tool, alerting us to situations or events that make us feel vulnerable. And with this awareness we can marshal our coping skills.

For example, if the idea of an upcoming exam makes us anxious, the tension and uneasiness can be a powerful motivator to study. Anxiety provides the opportunity to prepare for the event by anticipating the possible difficulties. Anxiety gives us the opportunity to *act* to protect ourselves in potentially difficult situations.

But for many people, anxiety can be experienced as a signal of impending doom, a flag that whatever is coming will be emotionally overwhelming. For most of us, we just try to make anxiety go away.

At 14, Carl was diagnosed with ARFID after years of being terrified of eating. He told us:

> *When I was a kid, I wasn't like the typical guy. I hated sports and was really shy. Anything new scared me. I think when I was nervous, I would get these awful stomach pains. The one thing that helped the pains was just not eating. It didn't matter that my parents got furious with me or that I kept getting skinnier and skinnier. It felt good not to eat. At least I didn't get sick. And then I realized that I had developed this hipster kind of cool look. I began to not mind being thin. I actually started to feel less nerdy.*

When someone you care about is in trouble with food or weight, pay attention to how anxiety is dealt with. If you sense that that person is anxious, how are they dealing with it? And what about you? If someone you care about is really anxious about something, it is easy to rush in and try to make their terror or angst go away. When this happens, a cycle of dependency is encouraged, if not completely cemented into the relationship. While everyone needs support at times, this kind of relationship can result in someone never having the confidence to listen to one's self and know one's own needs. When there is upset or trouble, the person scrambles to have someone else calm them down. When another person isn't around, food (or of course, vaping or drinking) can become the next likely substitute. Therefore, the experience of anxiety is often the trigger to binge or, as in the case of anorexia, to starve. While these behaviors numb the anxiety, they do nothing to help the person prepare for or protect against the actual cause of the anxiety.

AN EATING DISORDER IS A FORM OF SUBSTANCE ABUSE

In Rose's case, she was able to substitute a man for the food in order to define how she felt about herself and calm herself down. A man was a scale of sorts, telling her if she was good enough. He was also a warm, soothing body rather than a complex human being to interact with. In this way, a man was like a substance rather than a person. Be it a man or a binge, Rose was relying on an external substance to alleviate her inner distress. When used for emotional purposes, food functions similarly to a drug or alcohol: It provides escape.

As time goes on, food can replace people and the isolation increases. Said one 19-year-old coed who would binge and vomit several times nightly:

> It got to be so that I would rather spend a Saturday night eating than with my friends. Being with people felt superficial. I was just killing time till I could go home and eat. I'd be carrying on a perfectly normal conversation but in the back of my mind, all I'd be thinking about was all

*the food I could eat as soon as I left. I knew something
was wrong. I hated that food was so important, but I was
trapped. I couldn't get the thoughts of food out of my head
and I didn't know any way out.*

LONELINESS

When someone is constantly turning to outside sources to find
out who they are and how they should act, being alone can be
empty and terrifying. Eating (or sometimes starving) can tem-
porarily soothe this kind of painful experience.

Jim felt condemned to loneliness. His nightly binges felt
like his only escape. During the day, his self-consciousness
about his large body and weight kept him from taking part in
activities and events. He thought everyone would be as disgusted at the sight of him as he was when he looked at himself.

"When I'm at home alone," said Jim, "I get so lonely and it
becomes a physical emptiness inside. Planning what to eat becomes an activity—it's like planning whom I'll spend time with."

For some, loneliness is felt as boredom. This feeling can
occur despite the presence of other people. "I feel so lost," said
Maddie, who also spent many evenings bingeing:

*I'll be fine during the day, as long as I'm busy, but as soon
as I'm home at night, nothing seems to satisfy me. I feel
empty, lost, this sense of vague uneasiness. I try to read
or work but I feel distracted, ungrounded. I want to be
"filled up." I know my family is there and I can spend time
with them, but that doesn't do it for me. Sometimes drugs
or alcohol seem to take away that feeling. Other times,*

*if I sleep with a guy that might do it, too. But whether
it's food, drugs, guys, or booze, it's always temporary,
leaving me feeling horrible about myself afterward. And
empty still.*

These feelings are often intensified when people are in fact
alone. Some people experience being alone as though they
were abandoned, left behind. Thoughts of food or exercise
regimens—or even thoughts of starving—can be an oddly
satisfying kind of company at such empty times.

THEY MAY ALSO BE DEPRESSED

Many people with eating disorders grapple with low moods,
low energy levels, and feelings of despondency and sadness.

In some cases, the intensity of the mood and the seriousness of associated behaviors, such as severe sleep problems,
lack of interest in life, and constant self-deprecating thoughts
indicate the presence of a clinical depression.

Depression is usually associated with feelings of helplessness, ineffectiveness, loss of control, and/or unexpressed anger.
The more resilient, optimistic, or even fun-loving parts of the
person get lost. It feels like there is no way out. In these cases,
when depression is likely physiologically based, food can be
turned to in an attempt to alleviate or anesthetize the depression to make it bearable. In fact, bingeing can actually raise the
level of serotonin in the brain. Serotonin is a neurotransmitter
that can result in the feeling of well-being and calm. Thus for
some, bingeing may be an attempt at self-medication, a means
of providing temporary relief from dysphoric moods.[3]

For others, it is the out-of-control feelings about food and weight that can lead to depression. After all, how would you feel if you repeatedly promised yourself to stop some destructive, disruptive behavior and failed over and over again?

Moreover, both erratic and restrictive food intake can lead to internal chemical imbalances that can wreak havoc with mood. When this is the case, the mood swings and depressed feelings will be alleviated by a normal diet.

Sara spoke of her periods of extreme depression:

> *These waves of lethargy and dullness would come over me. The day before I'd be fine, but then I would wake up and feel such hopelessness and despair that there would be no point in going to work or seeing friends. What seemed to offer pleasure yesterday looked bleak and uninviting today. I couldn't move and I'd feel horrible about myself. I don't know what makes me feel like this. But once I start to feel this way, it goes on for weeks and there is nothing I want to do but eat. And then it lifts—as mysteriously as it began—leaving me 10 to 20 pounds heavier.*

Sara's depressions began years before the bingeing became a part of her life. She had a history of depressive episodes, but in childhood her depression manifested itself through sleep disturbances and crying spells. When Sara reached 11 or 12, she found that eating alone in her room seemed to comfort and calm her. Although she didn't know it, Sara's use of food was an attempt at medicating herself for a depression that no one knew existed. What started out as a naive attempt to deal with her depressive state quickly developed into bulimia.

Often, it is hard to know whether a depression has exacerbated disordered eating or whether the eating or restriction itself has resulted in mood change. Among the people for whom depression is associated with disordered eating, antidepressants and other medications can be a critical aspect of treatment. When there is any question at all, a professional consultation can help assess what would be needed next.

FEAR OF OTHERS

Even though disordered eating can lead to feelings of isolation, loneliness, and depression, for some, food still feels more comfortable than being involved with people. It can be hard to trust people; being close to someone threatens feelings of loss and disappointment. Some people fear losing themselves and their own identities in their attempts to please another person. Others fear that the other person will take over, dominating them and leaving them little room to be themselves. They want to feel closeness but need to push others away to feel safe. This dilemma makes being in a relationship with someone who is eating disordered endlessly exasperating!

Jody, who struggled with bulimia, had trouble letting others get near her for fear she would give up control, just as she had with her mother:

> My mom was always doing things for me. It could be anything from changing batteries in my radio to cleaning up my room. I guess she was just taking care of me, but I felt like she was controlling everything and I came to believe

I couldn't take care of myself. Now I worry about this whenever I get close to anyone else. I like being taken care of, but I quickly feel controlled. I'm so confused about this that the second I even make plans with someone I start to feel trapped.

SEXUALITY AND IDENTITY

Eating disorders are also linked to the worry about sexual intimacy. For some, sexual intimacy is one aspect of emotional relatedness that can be avoided through bingeing, weight gain, or even weight loss. Said Cindy, at age 34:

I was so afraid to let a man near me. Sex scared me. I never really felt sexual, even as a teenager or when I was in college. When I went into therapy though, my therapist wondered if I confused hunger for food with bodily hunger for sex. I literally had no idea. And I know I'm large. I always just assumed that men wouldn't be attracted to me because of my body. But recently I met this man who doesn't care about my weight. I really like him, but now I have even more to worry about. Will his feelings change? Will mine? Sometimes I think it was easier just to worry about eating and weight than it is to worry about getting close to this guy both in bed and out.

In our ever-changing culture, not only does sexuality and one's sexual orientation need to be considered, but gender questioning and fluidity is now part of the developmental process for many adolescents. We don't know what allows for someone's questioning of their gender. Again, social, psychological, and physical factors all contribute. But because this is new terrain, gender questions often result in complicated feelings, secrecy, and shame. And in that regard, gender dysphoria is also often associated with disordered eating.

Rafi had transitioned from female to male when he was in his early twenties. But the process of that transition was preceded by intense self-hatred for his female round and ample breasted body. Rafi told us:

> I think my earliest attempt to transition was actually by starving myself. When I was 12 and started to develop, I felt like my growing hips and chest made me feel so fat. The thinner I got, the closer I got to the body I wanted. Of course, within a year, I was basically starving and had to go to a residential program to gain weight. It was only there that I began to realize that food and weight were the least of my problems. I'm actually sort of glad I became anorexic. If I hadn't had the treatment I was in, I wonder how long the eating disorder would have disguised my turmoil about who I was in general.

All teens and young adults have questions about their identity. In fact, part of normal adolescence is to "try on" different roles and identities as a way of discovering who one is. But when normal developmental confusion is foreclosed by a sudden and fierce identity having mainly to do with food and body, there is clearly a problem at hand.

ANGER AND AGGRESSION

When feelings and/or identity need to be kept out of view, often there is a quiet anger at not being heard or understood.

Suzanne, 20, put it this way:

> In my house, I know my parents didn't mean it, but whatever my older brother said was golden. Somehow if I brought something up, the message was that I didn't know what I was talking about. My brother could argue with my parents but if I raised my voice, I was the "bitch." So now I don't even know what I feel anymore. I'm afraid if I say anything, it will be stupid and I hate conflict. Inside though, I think everyone else is stupid. It makes me so mad but I don't think anyone knows that.
>
> Sometimes I think the only way I get to be mad is when I'm eating. If anyone ever saw me, they wouldn't believe I'm the same person. When I binge, I'm in my own world and just doing what I want. I don't care about anyone else. If anyone saw me, it would be a disaster. But at least when I'm bingeing, no one gets hurt—except, I guess, me.

A child or teenager in conflict about her natural feelings of anger and aggression grows up to be an adult with equal difficulties. Only the context of her conflict broadens.

Jennifer, a 30-year-old corporate executive, describes how the requirements of her work clash head-on with her discomfort asserting herself:

It's bizarre—here I am in charge of a whole department and I'm uncomfortable with the idea of offending anyone, making anyone mad at me. Whenever I have to assert myself, which is often at this job, I feel like I've done something wrong. Then I go straight for the food. Somehow when I'm eating, I can forget about how badly it all makes me feel.

For anyone who worries what others think of them, the experience of anger or conflict can be very disruptive. Some people manage that experience by dissociating the anger from themselves. This means that they feel like they become someone else when they get angry or when they let out that anger through bingeing. As 19-year-old Liana told us:

It's like there is this horrible monster inside who takes over and I can't control it. When I'm in a bingeing phase, I'm like a different person. I'll be nasty and not care about others. Usually I'm a very nice person—too nice. Usually I'm the one who takes care of everyone else first and my own needs and feelings come last.

Other people have described this aspect of themselves as being "an ogre," a "derelict," or "it's the dark side of me." One patient suggested she was more in need of an exorcist than a therapist.

It is the "monster" that binges and thereby expresses parts of the person that feel bad, out of control, ugly, and distasteful. In the case of bulimia, this monster is undone by purging; in the case of anorexia, it is defeated by control. In either case, the feeling of being in a battle with oneself is a part of daily life.

Someone with an eating disorder usually has a great deal of trouble acknowledging, accepting, and enduring negative feelings like anger. But sometimes it is the more tender emotions, like affection, longing, and dependence that cause problems. These feelings can make someone feel vulnerable, too dependent, or scared. In either direction, feelings can be, and often are, intense. It is often easier to block them out then to risk their overwhelming one's self or, worse, others.

The fear of feelings can lead to panic and then a rush to food or restriction in a thwarted attempt to allow for peace.

NEEDS FOR APPROVAL AND NURTURANCE

But despite attempts to run from vulnerability, dependency and the need for others' approval often are center stage. Someone who is preoccupied with body shape and weight can dangerously rely on other people's opinions and reflections of them to remind them that they are okay. This is why criticism can be terrifying. Criticism not only means that something someone does or says is not approved of by others, but it can also be taken as a judgment about whether someone is a good or bad person.

As Jason, 25 years old and recovering from anorexia, told us, "If someone didn't like a shirt I wore, it didn't just mean that they didn't like the shirt—it meant they didn't like something about *me*. Like I was someone who would make a stupid mistake about how to dress." He had not yet learned how to rely on his own thoughts. Without confidence and self-compassion, he was dependent on others to give him the approval that he couldn't give himself.

Not only is approval needed, but inside, someone may be hungry for care and affection as well. When someone is so busy being attuned to everyone else's needs, their own may well have gotten overlooked. But wishing for others' care or attention can feel like weakness or failure. Often these feelings are disowned and avoided at all costs.

For some people, there is an intense fear that others will be overwhelmed by their needs and leave them or stop loving them. To avoid this, they try to be perfect inside and out. The strain is enormous.

Amy, who was well into her 30s, only recently began to see how this fear affected her life:

> I know it sounds crazy and isn't logical but I genuinely feel that to be loved I must be perfect. If a guy doesn't like me, I'm sure it's because I'm not thin enough, or my hair isn't nice enough, or I'm not smart enough. Then I have to work out, study harder, look better. It never occurs to me to think, "Do I like him?" All I can think about is that I'm not good enough.

The self-imposed demands of perfection and the fear of rejection interfere with the development of comfortable, intimate relationships. The dilemma is a difficult one. If someone can't reach out and allow one's self to need someone else, to be vulnerable to someone else, how can they really get to know that person and let themselves be known? And how can they ever leave the safety of food? Thinking about what to eat or what not to eat might be easier than thinking about what someone else can give you.

THE COMPLETE PICTURE

Because the symptoms of bingeing, vomiting, exercising, or starving can be so disruptive and frightening, it is easy to pay attention only to those behaviors. No question, anyone in trouble with food or weight will need direct help in managing the eating behaviors and normalizing health. But emphasizing the focus on food and weight misses the point. Overt eating disordered symptoms are just the tip of the iceberg. Beneath the surface lies a much larger piece of the picture—a complicated and complex world of feelings and experiences that are very much a part of the eating disorder. Not to question this would be akin to someone being treated for cancer and no one ever asking what effect the cancer was having on the person. Both the visible and invisible parts need to be acknowledged in order for someone with an eating disorder to be treated as a whole person, not just a symptom. Even if we find that anorexia is completely physiologically derived, the illness itself is still a critical opportunity to find out who that person is and what they may need in addition to just symptom abatement.

3.

RULES AND RELATIONSHIPS

The Family Context of Eating Disorders

WHEN SOMEONE IN A FAMILY DEVELOPS AN EATING DISORDER, IT IS AN opportunity to pay attention. Every family has its difficulties. Often it takes something going wrong to stop and evaluate what might need to change to better meet the needs of everyone involved.

We want to be clear that we are not saying that family rules can cause an eating disorder. Eating disorders are complex, and both physiologically and psychologically based. What is clear, however, is that once a family member does develop an eating disorder, that problem, in and of itself, generates stress for everyone and exacerbates whatever difficulties may have existed before. This, in turn, can result in the maintenance or the increase of disordered eating. The goal of paying attention to your family's rules and relationships is not to blame yourself but to notice what helps—and what doesn't—in terms of paving the way to recovery.

With any eating disorder, the goal is to help that person take hold of their own life, so that they are better able to make responsible choices regarding their own self-care and emotional awareness. It is not always clear how to help someone do this. In some cases, this will mean more active support, limit-setting, and structure. In other cases, it will mean backing off and letting go. In the worst of situations, it may mean accepting that someone has a disability greater than anyone can change, and that acceptance, connection, and love are still very much needed, no matter how serious the situation at hand. Every family differs in terms of what is needed—and each family's situation will continually change over time.

Families in which someone struggles with an eating disorder vary tremendously. In some families everything looks okay on the surface. In others the picture is overtly chaotic, with alcoholism, drug addiction, gambling, or family violence obvious to the onlooker.

However, in families in which a son or daughter has an eating disorder, there is often a common thread, one that gets exacerbated by the crisis of the eating disorder: The existing rules and practices that bind the family together are not accommodating the shifting needs of the individual members. The work in each family is to assess what is needed to help each person grow and change while still maintaining the family connections.

WHAT ARE FAMILY RULES?

In every family, rules evolve to help the family function. A family, in this regard, can also be any relationship—a marriage, a partnership, a close friendship. When we say *family*, we are talking about people connected by intertwined lives and love.

Family rules, which are often unspoken, have to do with

how to live together, how to express intimacy, how to disagree, and how to express needs. Family rules also dictate which feelings and behaviors are encouraged and which are met with disapproval. These rules are an attempt to provide everyone with a sense of belonging, a means of communicating, and a way of living together on a day-to-day basis.

There are many examples of family rules. The following are some that you might be familiar with: "Fighting is not allowed in this house." "The family that eats together stays together." "We tell each other everything." However, most rules are subtle and silently communicated and reinforced. They are learned ways of connecting with one another and protecting one's self that may not even be in anyone's conscious awareness.

These rules are attempts at ensuring safety, handling disagreement, fostering closeness, and expressing togetherness. In nuclear families, as children grow older, rules may be more overt and discussed. For example, later curfews and more privacy may be balanced with more household chores. Rules, at their best, allow for ongoing communication and a fine balance between freedom and responsibility. Family rules exist for parents as well. In some families, these rules can provide parents the opportunity to have a life of their own (that is, closing bedroom doors at night or going out without their children). In other families, the rules that are established can inhibit parents' freedom (i.e., bedroom doors are always open and babysitters are never hired). In relationships, rules can also allow for independence or constraint. If a rule in a relationship is that each person needs to know everything the other person is doing, this can allow either for closeness or suffocation, depending upon each person's needs.

Rules do not have to be spoken to be heard. Often, they

are conveyed via subtle messages that are adhered to rigidly and often unquestioned. A certain facial expression or physical posture can carry a great deal of meaning about what is or is not acceptable in a family.

The examples we give below are overt and sometimes extreme. Use them to think about your own family or relationship. What rules do you think you have carried with you to allow for connection or safety?

WHEN RULES DON'T WORK

In many families, rules that originally evolved to keep the family together end up inhibiting the growth and development of each member of the family—children *and* parents alike. Thus, when an eating disorder is involved, rules need to be questioned to make sure both the individual and the family itself keep moving forward in a road toward health.

In nuclear families, parents are not ill-intentioned when conveying family rules. The rules that develop are an attempt to help the family cope and get along together. Parents tend to bring the rules they learned during their own upbringing into their new families, thus perpetuating patterns of coping and relating throughout the generations. This transmission of patterns, however, can perpetuate less-than-ideal rules and practices.

Janie, 18, recovering from anorexia, recalled her surprise when she noticed that her grandmother treated her mother in the same way her mother treated her:

> *When we all went to visit Nanna for Christmas, her first words to my mother were, "Isn't that a bit too much*

makeup for you?" I'm sure this has always been going on, but I had never noticed it. My mother's face flashed anger and disappointment. I wondered if my mother realized that scene could just as easily have been of her talking to me.

In Janie's family, and in the family her mother came from, one clear but unspoken rule was that looks are important. Another rule, or pattern of relating, was that one person had a right to comment on someone else's looks or behaviors regardless of the person's age. In both families, however, the rules resulted in an accentuated focus on appearance, a feeling of being criticized, and an undermining of one's ability to decide for themselves how they should look.

In both families, these rules needed to be reevaluated, but it wasn't until Janie became anorexic and therapy was started that anyone imagined the family rules were keeping Janie dependent upon her mother's opinions to decide how she should look or feel. And this dependency in turn ended up inhibiting Janie from taking hold of her own recovery, from recognizing that she was fighting for her own life—not recovering for her mother.

Sometimes rules don't work because parents disagree about what the rules should be. The child does not get a clear message about what behavior is expected from them.

Rose, the young woman we mentioned earlier who used men and food for security, spoke to us about what it was like when her parents disagreed:

My parents could never agree about anything. My mother's story went back to when I was a baby. She felt it was important I be on a schedule—that I slept from seven p.m. to seven a.m., and that I ate at the same times every day. She said she would have had me trained at three months, but my father disagreed. He thought I could go to sleep easily if I were just held for a few minutes. He didn't understand how my mother could let me cry for such a long time. She would feel I was being manipulative and he was just going against her. My father felt my mother was cold and unfeeling. That fight in some form or other went on all my life.

It took looking at their different ways of acting to realize that only two things made me feel good—one was food and another was a man. My father was kind and comforting to me, but it would come at a big price. Whenever he took my side, my mother would stop speaking to me. So as a kid, I ate for comfort. I do the same thing now that I am older. I can only stop bingeing if I'm with a man.

One of the most common ways rules don't work has to do with parents' approaches to the eating disorder itself. Each parent brings to the situation rules he or she believes will stop the eating disorder. Often those rules differ and that's when trouble can occur. One of the most crucial aspects in dealing with an eating disorder is for parents to act together in their strategy toward their child and not be in conflict with one another.

When Max, 28, started to recover from a three-year history with anorexia, he described his situation this way:

When I became anorexic, my father kept saying, "I don't know what's wrong with you—just eat pizza like everyone else and everything will be all right. You look terrible—*your arms and legs are sticks, and all your clothes hang off of you.*"

My mother would disagree. She'd say, "*Max is having a rough time You can't make him eat. We need to find out what's going on inside of him. Just making him eat won't solve anything.*"

My father definitely did not buy that. He thought I just needed to be forced to eat. So they fought and I starved.

This may sound confusing but often when someone develops a symptom such as an eating disorder, it is that person's own way of fighting to evoke change. The person, however, is not someone who can fight openly; they are not a rebel. Thus, the fight is subtle and disguised. People often unwittingly hurt themselves when they know something is wrong but they just don't know what to do.

When the family can understand an eating disorder as a sign to question family rules and patterns or parental communications, the other problems have hope of resolution. This does not mean that medical and nutritional care and direct intervention won't be needed. But when families or couples adapt to changing needs in relationships by reevaluating rules, there is a much better chance that the eating disorder will take a transient, short-lived course as opposed to becoming embedded and ongoing in both the individual's and family's life.

Family-based treatment, the therapeutic approach in which parents are guided to directly feed their starving child, is based on the need for rules to change.[1]

Rules in families often have broken down when someone develops an eating disorder. The eating disorder, instead of parents, starts to rule the house. Food is hidden, heads are turned the other way, everyone walks on eggshells. Family-based treatment insists that rules are put into place—parents regain authority and there are consequences for not taking care of one's self. What we are urging is that the rules be rethought—not just in the arena of meals, food, and physical health, but in the arena of psychological health—for all family members—as well.

WHEN RULES AFFECT FEELINGS

Pearl was eight years old when her mother developed cancer. Her mother spent many years bedridden as Pearl, the only daughter, tended to her. Pearl's childhood was lost to her mother's illness, and as Pearl entered her teenage years without the freedom to date or enjoy after-school activities like the other teenagers, her anger and resentment understandably grew. At night, alone in bed and tearful, Pearl would wish that her mother would die so she could have her own life. When Pearl was 15, her wish was granted—but horror, not relief, followed. Maybe her mother had known of Pearl's anger. Maybe it killed her. Pearl's mother's death did not release her—it haunted her even through her own marriage and family life. In her family, Pearl made it clear that anger was to be avoided at all cost.

Pearl's experience with death and her fear of the consequences of anger pervaded her experiences with others. The effects of Pearl's experience influenced her daughter Emily, a 16-year-old high school student, recovering from anorexia nervosa.

Emily describes it this way:

> *Whenever I would get angry at my father and start to say anything, my mother would put her hand over her*

> *heart like she was warning me. This would stop me cold.*
> *I'd just stop what I was saying and leave. But I always*
> *felt angry and frustrated. The first time my mother*
> *didn't do that was when I was in the hospital and my*
> *parents thought I might die because I was so thin. Then,*
> *my mother was more frightened about my dying than my*
> *getting angry.*

Does this mean that Emily became anorexic because her family wouldn't let her be angry? Lots of families thwart anger—that doesn't mean someone will become anorexic. But once Emily was struggling with food, it was an opportunity to question whether she was also struggling with feelings. Being angry wouldn't cure Emily of her need to starve—but it could allow her the full range of feelings that are bound to come up during the recovery process. Recovery should not just mean weight gain. True recovery means awareness and acceptance of who one is, compassion for one's own struggles, and yes, the ability to know and express when one is angry or upset.

When family rules inhibit the experience or expression of feelings, the opportunities to accept and resolve these feelings are thwarted. Pent-up feelings may result in explosive episodes, in which release comes in a torrent of emotions that are uncontrollable and usually not productive. Pent-up feelings can also exacerbate physical illnesses, including stomach problems, back pain, colitis, and asthma. Or, they may lead to psychological symptoms as expressed in an eating disorder. When symptoms are the result of unexpressed feelings, it is important not just to focus on symptomatic change but also to learn how the symptom has been, potentially, a way to adhere to spoken or unspoken family rules. If someone is bingeing or starving, if they weren't thinking about food and weight, what would be on their mind?

The following passages describe common areas of trouble or concern.

EXPRESSION OF FEELINGS: "YOU'RE GOING TO KILL YOUR FATHER IF YOU SAY THAT"

The direct experience and expression of intense feelings such as anger, resentment, disappointment, jealousy, sadness, and loss are necessary for healthy functioning. In many families there is a rule, sometimes subtle, sometimes not, that these unpleasant feelings are to be avoided. Pearl's understanding of anger was that it could be dangerous.

Others may have come from families in which feelings actually did get out of control and resulted in violence. Certainly, rules inhibiting emotional expression would feel like life-protecting devices in this case. For some people expressing painful feelings is a sign of weakness. In any of these situations, when rules develop that stop the natural expression of feelings, finding effective and modulated means of expressing them seems impossible.

Keith, 42, had grown up in a strict religious family. In his family, one unquestioningly respected one's elders and most displays of emotion were strongly discouraged. His own upbringing influenced how he raised his daughter Maureen.

Maureen describes it this way:

> My mother died when I was six years old and my father remarried when I was 10. As soon as he married my

stepmother, all the pictures of my mother were taken off the living room walls. I didn't mind that so much, but then my father made me put away all the pictures of my mother that I had in my bedroom. I'd have to sneak away to look at them. Sometimes I'd ask questions about my mother and my father would give me a confused look and just not answer. Over time, I developed a ritual that I guess made me feel like I was still with my mom. I would buy lots of sweets and gather all the pictures I had of my mother, close my bedroom door, block everything else out, and be with my mom and eat.

Keith was not trying to be mean to his daughter. It was just that he himself had never expressed his own feelings of sadness and loss as a child. Now as an adult, faced with the traumatic loss of his wife, he turned to the familiar rules of his family: "Pull it together," "Don't think about it," and certainly "Don't let it show." Naturally, Maureen abided by these same unspoken rules. Food became the only safe outlet for the loneliness and sadness she felt about her mother.

EXPRESSION OF CONFLICT: "OUR FAMILY NEVER FIGHTS"

One of the reasons that families avoid direct expression of intense feelings is that they fear conflict among family members. If people say what they feel, they may not agree with each other and tension, arguing, and conflict will result. To some, conflict calls into question the family's closeness; it is interpreted to mean that people do not love one another. Complaining or disagreeing threatens the bonds of the family. Therefore, a high value is placed on everyone getting along well. The rule, then, often unspoken, is that one doesn't behave in ways that may cause conflict.

Such a rule, designed to keep the family close, may have consequences for the children. When there is no acceptable way to disagree and be different, there is no way for someone to learn to trust and value their own experiences.

ASSUMING AND ASCRIBING FEELINGS: "YOU MUST BE HUNGRY"

When open communication is inhibited (even if this is done unwittingly), family members are left to guess or assume what the others feel. When assumptions about feelings are made, children grow up without the opportunity to learn about, trust, and communicate their own feelings.

Kerry, 22 and struggling with bulimia, brought this issue up in her support group:

> My parents spent my childhood telling me what they thought I was feeling instead of ever asking. They weren't trying to be mean or anything. It's just that they'd say things like, "It's 42 degrees. You must be cold" or "I know you must be hungry." I'd always know from their questions what they'd want me to say and I'd answer that way—I hated to let them down. I also think I believed that they really knew what I wanted better than I did. The problem is that I'm not sure what I want. My insides seem like a puzzle—I don't even know what food I'm hungry for let alone what I'm feeling.

Every family has its share of miscommunications and misunderstandings. It is unclear whether problems with feelings actually cause an eating disorder. But once an eating disorder is in the picture, it is very clear that problems with feelings can keep someone from knowing what to do instead of eating or starving. Finding the tools to know what is going on inside is always a critical part of the work toward recovery.

WHEN RULES DON'T SHIFT: PROBLEMS GROWING UP

Another common problem in families is that rules do not flexibly shift in response to family members' ages, needs, and capabilities. For children in particular, flexible rules are necessary to allow for natural dependence while encouraging increasing autonomy. This enables children to test their expanding capacities in a safe environment that allows for failure while parents are still available to help.

The transition from being the parents of young children, where watchfulness and protectiveness are necessary for the child's survival, to being the parents of adolescents, where this watchfulness needs to decrease, is a difficult one for many families. It is a shift that requires parents to allow the teenager to try things on their own even when the parents know a better way. When parents are able to make this shift, the children develop an increasing sense of their own competency and ability to negotiate the demands of the outside world. When parents have difficulty shifting rules or disagree about what the rules should be, or when rigid and fixed rules do not allow for independent behavior, kids may fight for these changes in indirect ways. Withdrawal from the family, the use of drugs or alcohol, the refusal to eat or eating secretly are among the behaviors resorted to when a child feels helpless and controlled.

While these behaviors may allow for a feeling of independence, they do so at a high cost. They limit the child's natural and healthy capacities to grow up and achieve a life independent of one's parents, and instead leaves them with a destructive method of asserting one's self.

Remember, these rules don't necessarily create an eating disorder. But the eating disorder is an opportunity to question what rules are working—and what aren't—in your family.

WHEN RULES INHIBIT FREEDOM

Jenette was 16 when her mother brought her into therapy for bulimia. "She just binges all night long, Doctor. I buy food for the family and it's gone by morning. Then she's in the bathroom at all hours of the night getting rid of it."

Jenette saw the problem differently. "That may be what's upsetting you, but I'm suffocating. You never let me stay out with my friends. I have to be in at 10 p.m. on the weekends. All my friends stay out later. I'm always the one who has to leave the parties. You don't trust me, but you've never given me a chance."

Jenette's parents were first-generation Americans from Eastern Europe. They were fearful of what problems freedom could bring to teenagers. Drugs were rampant in Jenette's school and one of her friends had already had an abortion. These parents were not going to let that happen to their daughter. But Jenette did not feel protected by her parents' rules. The only thing she felt was that she was being punished—and for no reason. At night while she sat at home, feeling lonely and resentful, the frustration was overwhelming. Eating and purging allowed her to calm her feelings—but at the cost of finding more appropriate ways of developing her independence and taking hold of her life.

WHEN BOUNDARIES AND PRIVACY ARE SACRIFICED

All families create boundaries to allow for privacy, independence, increased control, and a sense of separateness. Just the way people create boundaries around the land they own so no one will trespass, there are boundaries around people. There are individual boundaries for each person and boundaries around groups of people, such as with spouses or siblings.

When the family has difficulty establishing, maintaining, and respecting boundaries, problems develop. People can feel intruded upon. The most extreme boundary violation is incest, where a child's own body is not safe from intrusion. A less extreme occurrence is when a parent enters a teenager's room without permission and goes through their possessions or reads their private journals. Boundaries, especially those that have to do with privacy, also need to shift as children grow up.

Often boundary violations can be emotional and not easy to pinpoint. As we saw in families where feelings are ascribed and not expressed, a child may not learn to be comfortable as an individual separate from her parents, with different ideas, thoughts, and feelings.

Marcia, a 24-year-old who suffered from anorexia nervosa, talked about living in her family:

> *I always felt confused when I was growing up. My mother would use the word "we" whether she was talking about me or about herself. Someone would ask how I was and*

she would say, "We're fine." I had trouble figuring out
what were my feelings and what were hers.

One of the ways in which parents set a boundary between themselves and their children is by establishing rules. When parents make rules, they are assuming a position of authority and creating a structure in the family that permits children to feel protected and independent.

For some parents, the position of authority is difficult to assume. They want to feel close to their children and fear that if they set limits their children will get angry and not love them. This type of closeness can make it hard for the child to become independent. If a child is made to feel like the friend of a parent, rather than the child, they do not have the opportunity to separate from the family and develop meaningful relationships apart from the parents.

Rachel, 24, and her mother, Elise, were best friends. They spent lots of time together, and told each other everything. Rachel felt lucky to have a mother who was so much fun. It was only with her mother that her large body did not make her feel bad about herself.

The trouble came when Rachel met a man she liked. She had rarely dated during college but now there was Richard, someone who was also interested in her. As Rachel and Richard began to spend time together, Rachel noticed she didn't feel like calling her mother every day.

When Rachel didn't call Elise, Elise felt scared. She had gone from her parents' home to her husband, and then to her daughter when her husband left. Elise had never been alone. She would call Rachel several times a day. Sometimes she would ask if Rachel had forgotten she had a mother. Rachel would then insist to Richard that her mother come with them on different weekend outings. Richard resented this and it led to many arguments between them.

After a few months of this, Richard ended the relationship. He was tired of having Rachel's mother be so much a part of their relationship. Rachel, upset and torn between closeness to her mother and her relationship with Richard, contacted us for therapy.

Rachel was having trouble developing a private, independent life without feeling as though she was deserting her mother. She even started to wonder if staying ashamed about her body size kept her closer to home. Rachel's mom would never have thought she was intruding on Rachel's boundaries. All Elise wanted was to make sure that her small family of two stayed close.

Boundary difficulties can appear in many forms. They can be subtle, such as in the case of Rachel and her mom, or more problematic, such as secretly reading someone else's emails. The worst possible sort of boundary violation with the worst consequences for the victim is sexual violations. Reports of sexual abuse and incest within the eating-disordered population vary tremendously, with research indicating that anywhere from 4 to 65 percent of patients have been sexually abused.[2]

But even the most subtle of boundary questions arise when someone in the family has an eating disorder. "Should I be monitoring my daughter's computer?" one mother asked. "I know she is going on those sites that encourage kids to starve." Or what about going through someone's drawers if you are worried that they are hoarding food and bingeing? Can you read someone's diary if you are worried?

If something is obvious—vomit on the toilet, food missing, a diary left open in a family room—this may well be a message that the person in trouble wants someone to know but doesn't know how to talk about it. If something is there for you to see, it's okay to look.

But privacy is important in any relationship, so do not go looking for things that you can't see. If there is a problem, there will be many things you can notice without having to prove that a problem exists. Weight gain or weight loss will tell you more than finding candy stored in someone's bedroom drawer. Time on the computer and social isolation will again say more than the actual content of what an internet search will reveal. And of course, rules will differ depending on someone's age. For example, internet content and social media should indeed be monitored for children. As kids grow older though, privacy should be allowed with more focus on talking about what is being found (remember, if someone can't do a search on the home computer, they certainly will find a way to do that search somewhere else).

The most important rule of thumb is to talk about any concern you have. In Chapter 5 we'll discuss how to bring up uncomfortable conversations. For now, if you find yourself being a secret agent, looking to find something you haven't yet seen, question why you are doing that. The concern that you have is what needs to be discussed.

WHEN RULES ARE UNPREDICTABLE: CHAOTIC FAMILIES

In some families, difficulties arise because the rules are changeable, confusing, and unpredictable. As a result, the child learns to depend on one's self, not on the stability of the family, and independence may come too soon, leaving the child fearful and anxious. They may turn to food to calm anxiety—or refuse it to make one's self feel stronger.

In families where the rules are chaotic or unstable, drug or alcohol abuse may be part of the family picture. When parents are involved with alcohol or drugs, they cannot provide a stable family structure and consistent rules for the child. These families often function from crisis to crisis. The household can be disorganized and the children are often left with responsibilities that would otherwise be in the hands of parents. A child or adolescent in such a position is left feeling inadequate. They do not have the resources or abilities to cope with all the problems that occur in filling the gaps. While they may appear to be functioning well, this is often a precocious independence and an autonomy built on sand.

It took Scout, 15, months to speak to their support group:

> *I don't know what it's going to be like when I come home from school. If she's had a "good" day, she's a lot of fun. She'll ask me how my day was, she'll suggest we make dinner together or go shopping. But if she's been drinking (which lately is more often than not) she'll have passed out on the couch with the TV blaring. Then I know if I don't shop for dinner and cook, my two younger sisters and I won't eat. Even when she wakes up, she's so groggy that it's up to me to get my sisters to do homework and get to bed. At around 11 p.m., the house is quiet and I can finally get to my homework. I'm just scared I can't keep it up. Last week I got my first C ever. This is getting to me.*

What Scout didn't tell the group until two months later was how food fit in. "At night when it's quiet, when I'm doing my homework I eat. All night sometimes. But I'm scared of gaining weight so that's why I started taking laxatives. It started at one or two but now I can take 50 at a time before they work."

When substance abuse exists among parents, strong messages are communicated about experiencing and conveying feelings—in particular, that you can numb your feelings and that pain or upset will not go away on its own. The children hear a clear message: Feelings are unmanageable and substances help.

WHEN RULES FOCUS ON APPEARANCE

In many families in which eating disorders occur, there is a very high value placed on appearance. Rules about how one looks are as powerful as rules about how one behaves. This doesn't mean that paying attention to looks and health can cause an eating disorder. In fact, if a parent eats healthfully or watches one's weight, this will not necessarily result in an eating-disordered child. However, constant self-deprecating remarks about bulging thighs or repeated talk about the need to lose weight can send the message that thinness is to be prized above all else. If attention to looks is an ongoing and much discussed concern in the family, then pressure to maintain perfection can prevail and disordered eating and body image are at risk.[3]

In this regard, in some families, looking good is synonymous with being worthwhile. Audrey, 24, described it this way:

When I walk in the door to greet my parents, the first thing they say is, "Oh, you look great—you've lost a few pounds" or "Did you cut your hair? It looks shorter." The worst thing is when they won't say anything. Then I know that they think I've gained weight or don't look so good and they don't want to hurt my feelings. It's ridiculous but now if someone I'm with doesn't say I look good, I think they're being critical of me.

No question commenting on looks is part of our culture, particularly among women. "You look so good! Did you lose weight?" often replaces "hello" when two women meet. In families, the question is not whether looks are noticed, but whether a focus on looks supersedes attention to other aspects of who the person is.

Kurt, 26, was in treatment for alternately bingeing and restricting when he spoke about his parents' preoccupation with appearance:

My parents were always talking about food and weight. It seemed like both of them were on a new diet every other week. At dinners I would hear "All anyone in this family has to do is look at food and they gain weight."

Last year, my girlfriend and I got engaged. But, as a total shock to me, she suddenly broke off the engagement—and ended up going out with a friend of mine. I just withdrew, I couldn't talk to anyone and, during that time, I couldn't stop eating. Before the breakup, in anticipation of the wedding, I was doing these Spartan workout regimens and juicing. My body looked great. But now I was alone

again, kicked out of my girlfriend's apartment, and back
living with my family. I could barely get out of bed and,
of course, started to look pretty bad. I think I gained 15
pounds in a few weeks. I know my mother was worried
that I wouldn't meet someone else so I guess she focused
on the only thing she could control. But whenever she had
a chance to talk to me, all she'd talk about was whether
I should get on a weight loss program as a way of pulling
myself together. I know she meant the best, but honestly,
she asked more about my stomach than she did about
how I was doing.

Kurt's mother was not ill-intentioned. She was only trans-
mitting the rules about appearance that she had grown up
with. She herself was an attractive woman, and her attractiveness was a quality for which she was often praised and ad-
mired. Her focus on looks was not meant to hurt Kurt but was
an attempt at encouraging a quality that she thought would be
helpful to her son.

Another reason why appearance is so highly valued in
some families is that some parents feel responsible for how
their child looks or behaves, responsible in a way that over-
rides the child's right to determine how they look or what they
eat. Parents are almost always well-intended. For example, no
parent wants a son or daughter (particularly a daughter) to be
overweight. In our culture, that's a sure risk for being bullied or
being an outcast. Parents are worried and try to help, but often
at an unwitting cost.

For years, at almost catastrophic levels, kids who have
gained weight or who are in larger bodies have been put on di-

ets. Parents have thought that certainly this would be the best way to care for their son or daughter. But here's the problem—diets don't work! Approximately 95 percent of all diets fail and 66 percent of kids and adults who diet ultimately, once the diet is broken, gain more weight than when they started. In the case of a child, often well-intentioned helping just ends up hurting.[4]

Allowing a growing child or teen to take agency over their own life healthfully and responsibly is likely the hardest task of parenting. In the arena of food, the role of good parenting in this regard has drastically changed. For example, Health at Every Size (HAES) is a research-based, weight-neutral approach to health that strongly discourages dieting and, instead, encourages both body acceptance and a better understanding of one's physical and emotional needs.

The Ellyn Satter Institute provides another research-oriented approach in which the goal again is allowing children and teens to best know what their bodies need. Here, the parenting work allows for a division of responsibility in which parents make decisions regarding what, when, and where feeding occurs. But it is up to the kids to determine how much one eats—or whether to eat at all. This approach means parents do indeed monitor eating in between meal or snack times, but meals themselves are oriented toward helping kids take responsibility and agency over their own bodies and what they eat, ideally allowing kids to grow into the body that is right for them.

In general, rules about appearance are changing. Body acceptance is on the rise because body hatred has resulted in an epidemic of eating disorders. Notice the rules in your house.

When you try to help your daughter or son, is it indeed help-ing? Or are you unwittingly hurting your child with quiet (or not quiet) messages that your child isn't okay the way he or she is?

The work is to encourage kids to know their internal hun-ger cues, satiety, and appetite. Healthy habits need to be en-couraged that allow for health and well-being, not just weight control. And importantly, kids need to understand and cope with internal feelings so that food isn't repetitively used to quell difficult emotions. How one feels is as important as what one eats when it comes to kids and food. A focus on appearance not only misses the point, it completely misses the kid and sets the stage for serious problems in which food and weight become, ongoing, a troubled part of that person's life.

THE RULES

When someone in a family develops an eating disorder, the first step is to evaluate the unspoken rules in the family and question how they may need fine-tuning. For many of you reading this chapter, the examples will feel extreme, far from your own family experiences. If that is the case, a more nu-anced and detailed look at your family's interactions would be needed. Sometimes the most subtle of gestures communi-cate rules—an eye roll, a tone, trying to fix a problem when someone just needs to be heard. What is needed will vary tre-mendously from family to family. For example, sometimes this will mean modifying family interactions so that someone is not always dependent on others to tell them who to be and what to feel. For others, it may mean that parents take more control and assert their authority more steadily. In each case, how the family attends to someone's disordered eating—and to one another—will differ. Pay close attention to what may be needed in your family, friendship, or relationship. It won't always be clear and often takes some close listening to be able to tell what is helpful—and what is not.

PART II

CONFRONTING THE PROBLEM

4.

NO MORE SECRETS

Bringing It Out in the Open

IF YOU SUSPECT OR KNOW THAT SOMEONE IS EATING DISORDERED, ONE of the first questions you will probably ask yourself is whether you should say anything to the person you're worried about. And if you do speak to them, what should you say?

If you think someone is in trouble, this is no time for secrets. If the person does not know you are worried about them, the first thing you must do is tell them. Silence at these times will at best continue the discomfort and at worst lead to a dangerous and serious problem being ignored. No change can occur without first breaking the silence.

PLANNING TO TALK

Bringing up the subject of an eating disorder is never an easy task, but if done with some planning and forethought, difficulties and embarrassments can be minimized. What you say can potentially influence the course of the person's recovery. You will need to anticipate how you should approach the subject, what will be said, who will say it.

This chapter will help you anticipate what will happen in the discussion and will offer effective guidelines. By planning the discussion in advance, you can ease the discomfort and anxiety you are inevitably feeling and, by being prepared, you will have the best chance of being understood.

HOW TO APPROACH THE PROBLEM

Use the following guidelines before speaking with the person you're concerned about.

1. Think through who the best person is to do the talking.

   If you are a parent with a partner, both of you should be present to signal that you are both concerned. You can decide who would have an easier time talking without any party getting upset, but it's important to give the message that you both are involved. Don't involve the rest of the family until after speaking with your son or daughter privately. If parents don't live together, make sure both parents still give the message that they each are concerned.

   If you are a sibling and concerned about your sister or brother, you may want to speak with them privately or you may want your parents to do so. If your sibling is a minor or you are a minor, your parents really need to know what's going on.

   If you are a spouse or in a relationship, it is your responsibility to speak with your partner. You can discuss together if anyone else needs to be told. Respect privacy, and do not speak with friends, in-laws, or others until you speak with your partner.

If you are a friend or roommate, you should be the person to do the talking initially. Do not go to authorities or family until you have spoken with your friend first. In a house in which there are several roommates, a house meeting can be called in which anyone affected by the problem can participate. In the latter case, only one person should initiate the discussion, so that there will be less likelihood of the person feeling attacked by everyone at once.

If you are the son or daughter, you may be in the most difficult situation of all in terms of talking to your parent. Does your parent have a partner who can join you in the conversation? If not, find a calm time to talk alone with your parent. As in the case with anyone, the message you want to give is that you don't want to look back and feel like you ignored someone in trouble—even if this is your mom or dad.

2. Pick a time to talk when you are feeling calm.

Do not try to bring up this subject when you are angry, upset, or hurt. If you are upset, your pain may be burdensome to the other person—it may be harder for them to open up if they fear causing you even more pain. In addition, your feelings may interfere with your achieving the goals that you have in mind. Do not bring up your concerns in the middle of a fight. Accusations, confrontations, and pleas to change will only result in shutting down potential lines of communication. The other person is likely to end up being defensive and will perceive your concerns as a criticism or an attack. If someone is defensive, they certainly will not be open to hearing you out at that time.

3. Pick a time to talk when you know you won't be interrupted.

For example, don't start such a discussion 10 minutes before you have to go to work or you will feel very pressured. This pressure can make things go badly. The time limit may discourage the other person from opening up to you because of a fear of being cut off. Both of you must know you have as much time as is needed to talk.

4. Consider writing down what you want to say ahead of time.

It is inevitable that you will feel anxious or worried when you start to talk; that is natural and to be expected. By familiarizing yourself with what you want to say before you actually say it, you will be clearer when you do speak and your anxiety may be lessened. You'll also be sure to remember everything you want to say once you start talking. There are three things you will need to address in the discussion: (1) what your worries are, (2) how you feel, and (3) what you would like the outcome of the discussion to be.

WHAT IS WORRYING YOU?

When you discuss your concerns, you need to explain why you have come to suspect a problem. You will want to be specific about what you see with regard to the eating, purging, exercising, starving, or weight-related behaviors. If you have noticed changes that affect your relationship, you will need to point these out as well. Use the information from the checklists in Chapter 1 to help you clarify what it is you see or suspect.

When you have the discussion, you are going to have to be as direct and frank as you can. For example, as hard as it is to say, "I hear you vomiting," this is much more honest than, "I think you spend a lot of time in the bathroom." If you say the latter, you are leaving the door open for the problem to get ignored or denied. The implied message is, "I really don't want to talk about this either." If you are open in your approach, you are saying, "I know this is embarrassing but I want to be of help—let's address this problem head-on for what it is."

You are going to have to be careful not to make this an indictment of what you see. Your observations should not be listed as evidence of wrongdoing, but should be discussed gently as bases for your concern. This is a subtle distinction that has to do with tone and approach but one that can make all the difference in the world.

During your talk, you will have to stick to the issue and keep yourself from becoming distracted. If the person you are worried about changes the subject, tell them you'd like to find some time to speak about these other matters, but for now you don't want to avoid the problem at hand. You should let them know that *you* know this is a hard problem to discuss but that you don't want to let the issue get sidetracked.

WHAT DO YOU FEEL ABOUT IT?

When planning what you will say, include letting the person know what your experience is. One way to do this is to use what are called "I" statements. "I" statements are statements that focus on your own feelings and experience, not that of the other person.

Merely using the word *I* does not make for an "I" statement. "I think there's something wrong with you," and "What is the matter with you? I wonder what kind of person eats all that food and then throws up?" are *not* "I" statements. They focus on the other person and will be heard as attacking or blaming.

An "I" statement involves talking about yourself. "I've been worried about what I'm seeing. I haven't known whether to approach you or not, but I'm feeling too worried not to say something," or "The missing food is making me really angry. I don't like walking around being so mad at you. I want to find some way of working this out."

We are not suggesting you negate your own anger, frustration, or hurt. You are in an upsetting situation and will naturally have many reactions to this. However, merely venting feelings will only result in the person's becoming defensive and your being shut out. We are encouraging you to express your feelings in a way that you will be heard.

Using "I" statements does not mean you can't talk about the other person. Of course, you will need to tell them why you are worried and what you perceive the problem to be. ("I've heard you vomiting," or "You keep mentioning how worried you are about your weight lately.") But it is important to avoid telling the person how you think *they feel*. For example, avoid making statements like, "You must be very angry or you wouldn't be doing this." Resist judging the other person's experience. This will decrease the possibility of the other person's feeling attacked or controlled and will increase the success of your conversation.

WHAT ARE YOUR GOALS?

The third area that you should think through is what you would like to accomplish in this discussion. Be sure your goals are realistic and attainable.

IMPOSSIBLE GOALS

If your goal in approaching someone is to get them to stop bingeing, purging, or starving—STOP! While soon you may well have to set limits or take charge (particularly if your child is in any medical danger), it would be premature to do so at this first stage. This is an impossible task and you will fail in your attempts. Indeed, if you are coercive you may unwittingly encourage the other person to be more secretive and less talkative. You will most likely end up in a control battle and make matters worse. For anyone, bringing the problem out in the open is a beginning stage in the process of recovery. The first goals have to be clear, small, and contained.

REALISTIC GOALS

Opening the Doors to Talk

You will want to let the other person know that they can talk with you and that you want to be there for them in any way you can. Let them know that you don't want to look back in a year or two and feel like you turned away even though you were worried that they were having a hard time.

Helping Them Get the Help They Need

Sometimes, it will turn out that the person knows there is a problem and has already sought help. This might be likely if you are talking with a friend or spouse. Then the goal would be to figure out whether you can be of support in any way.

However, more often, the person may deny that anything is wrong. If this is the case, then the most important goal would be to help them get an evaluation to determine if a problem exists and if so, what needs to be done next. In this situation, tell them that maybe nothing is wrong, but if indeed there is a problem, you don't want to be the kind of person who pretends a good friend or family member is okay when you think they are in trouble. Offer your help in finding a suitable professional who can do an evaluation. If you are the parent of a child or adolescent, you will have to do the work to arrange for a treatment consultation. Your son or daughter should know that the family will be seeking help so that if there is a problem, indeed it can be addressed. If your parent is the person with the eating issues, find out if you can speak to their therapist if they are already in treatment. Eating disorders affect the whole family, particularly the kids. The therapist should want to know what's happening at home. If your mom or dad isn't getting help, suggest you go together to see what, if anything, is needed. With a parent who insists that nothing is wrong, it may be up to you to find the support you need on your own.

Changing How the Eating Disorder Is Affecting You

While the most important goals are opening the door to talking and beginning to assess what help may be needed, often there are more mundane issues that have been building up that also need to be addressed. Realistic goals may be to change how the eating behaviors have been affecting day-to-day living in your household or relationship. Roommates talk to us about the frustration of food missing from the kitchen. Siblings are angry that there is vomit on the toilet. Parents consistently talk about their daughter's belligerent or depressed attitude when food is around—mealtimes have devolved into stressful battlegrounds. In these cases, some goals of talking may be to make specific changes regarding how the eating behaviors interfere at home. We will be talking about how to handle these kinds of situations in the following chapters.

In any of these situations, do not expect that the goals will be accomplished right away. It is very important to take small steps and not focus too far ahead. For now, all you want to do is think about what needs to change. For example, if you need to discuss how food is handled in the house, don't try to work it out immediately. Set up another time to do this. Everything does not have to be worked out in one discussion. Or if the other person isn't worried about the eating problems that you see, don't try to argue with them. Start by just listening. Try to understand how they see things. Only once you better understand the other person's experience can you proceed to the next step of knowing what needs to be changed and figuring out whether more help is needed.

GIVING IT YOUR BEST SHOT

1. You can practice the discussion with someone.

   This may seem unnecessary but it is surprising how many people enter into very serious conversations without really thinking through what they want to say or what might go wrong. Anticipating the talk will certainly help to avert a disastrous interaction. If there is a family member or friend who is aware of the eating problem, you can practice what you'd like to say before the discussion is actually held. Tell that person what it is you want to say. Ask them to respond by saying the type of difficult responses you think you will get. This way, you'll have had time to anticipate some of the difficult spots and when the real situation occurs, you'll be more prepared to handle it. If there is no one else who is aware of the problem, respect the other person's privacy. There are many online services in which you can speak to a professional or someone in recovery who can help you know what's best to say. (See Chapter 6 for more information regarding support resources)

2. You can stop the conversation before it gets out of control.

   Keep this in mind when thinking about what you will say. This discussion is most likely going to be difficult and, if you are not careful, can lead into a battle of wills. Remember, it will be up to *you* to keep the conversation from becoming a fight, no matter what the reaction of the other person is. Let your concern show. If you find, though, in the discussion that you become angry or upset, STOP THE CONVERSATION before it gets heated and hurtful. You should tell the person that you want to continue talking at a time when you are not so upset. Tell them you'd like to try again, maybe under different circumstances or with someone else present.

It is not necessary that everything be said at once. You will have made a start. Continuing when emotions are heated will only make things worse. It is okay to try again at another time.

3. If you are worried that the situation is urgent or an emergency, you will need professional guidance as to how to proceed.

Tell the person that you are concerned enough that you need to have a professional evaluate the situation and give advice as to what to do next. Read "No Time to Waste: Emergency Situations" in Chapter 5 for more information as to what to do now.

ANTICIPATING REACTIONS

You cannot easily predict how someone is going to respond to your overtures. A variety of reactions is possible and your response will vary depending on what happens. The following sections detail some of the reactions that people commonly have when they are approached about an eating problem.

RELIEF

For some, knowing that someone else is aware of the problem affords great relief. They're not alone anymore with their secret and now there's someone to help them.

Seventeen-year-old Joanna referred to her discussion with her mother this way:

> After my mother told me that she knew I was bulimic and that she wanted to help me, I felt calm for the first time in a year. I could stop pretending everything was all right with me. I could talk to my parents about some of my feelings. I had been so worried that if my mother found out, she wouldn't be able to take it. Now I didn't have to think about that anymore.

Expressed relief may actually come much later, even years after the confrontation. Marianne, 18, looks back to when she was 15 and her parents insisted that she see a doctor because she had lost so much weight:

> I remember screaming at the top of my lungs—no way was I going to someone. I was terrified my parents would make me gain weight. I hated them and I told them so. They didn't know what was best for me.
>
> Only now can I admit that I also remember this other feeling underneath saying, "You can stop now. You don't have to fight anymore." Everything felt quiet inside for the first time in a long time, like a life preserver had been thrown out to me. I remember I just started to cry.

ADMISSION OF A PROBLEM

Sometimes once someone realizes other people are aware of the problem, the person is able to admit something is really wrong. Shelly, a 19-year-old college junior, binged and vomited every night after classes. Because she and her roommate, Dara, lived in such close quarters, she was sure Dara knew. Even though Shelly never ate or threw up in front of her roommate, Shelly knew Dara saw the food and smelled the bathroom odors. As Shelly puts it:

> Dara was pretty thin herself, so I just figured she thought the bulimia was not such a bad thing—like I had a good trick to lose weight. But one night, Dara told me that she knew I was bulimic and that she was really upset about it. She said she thought I needed help. I was shocked. I had thought all along that she didn't think it was so bad. When she said this to me, I was embarrassed and, for the first time, really worried. It was like I finally had to look at what I was doing. Up until then, I thought maybe it wasn't so bad if Dara didn't think so. It was only after that night that I realized I was in trouble and should go for help.

Some of you may have the fortunate experience of broaching the subject and finding that the person you are worried about is not only aware of the problem but is already in treatment. An important goal has already been achieved and the road has been paved for an open discussion. (Move on to Chapters 7, 8, and 9.)

DEFENSE AND DENIAL

Not everyone confronted about an eating disorder will react like the teens just described. You may find that the person you're approaching denies that a problem exists. Someone in the depth of anorexia will most likely deny that they have a problem and they'll do everything they can to convince you that they don't. They'll say they feel fine, they are healthy, that it's not a problem. Someone struggling with bingeing and/or purging will likely feel nothing but shame in being found out. Relief is the last thing on their minds at that moment. Remember, you may be the first person talking to them about a secret they may have harbored for years. Your concern may be met with any one of a variety of angry responses.

"HOW DARE YOU!"

The person may get furious at you. They may feel intruded upon, embarrassed, found out, and they will react defensively to keep you away. They'll tell you there is no problem—they don't know what you are talking about. Be prepared for this possibility—no one likes being confronted with a shame-filled secret. It's important for you to remember that anger is a normal response to the subject you're bringing up. The anger is masking embarrassment, shame, and fear, and at this stage of the game, the person may think you are trying to take something away from them.

Be prepared. If you anticipate an angry scene in advance, you'll be better equipped to react to it without getting upset yourself. Don't be intimidated by what the person says. No matter what they are saying, they may very well need you at this point. (Remember Marianne, who could only years later admit her relief at being found.) Hold your position and repeat why you are concerned. Remember, no matter what the person says, this is not a time for *you* to react angrily, too. It's likely you'll feel angry but this is not the time to express it.

"MIND YOUR OWN BUSINESS"

The person may tell you it's not your business. It's their life and they can do what they want. They will tell you you're always butting in and that if you stopped worrying, maybe they wouldn't have a problem in the first place. They'll tell you they can handle things on their own. In this case, tell the person you care about how their problem *is* affecting you and how they've made it your business. Be careful, though. It's one thing to explain how the problem is affecting you, what needs changing; it's another thing to sound accusatory. If you are a close friend, family member, or partner, you might tell them what they have done to make you worry, like losing a frightening amount of weight, bingeing, or never going out anymore. Tell them they can't expect someone who cares about them to ignore them. If you live with the person whom you think is in trouble, perhaps they've regularly eaten all the household food or spent long hours in the bathroom when you want to use it. That is certainly your business. Most importantly, let them know that it affects you because it scares you. You're scared that a part of them may be in trouble. Again, you don't want to look back in five years and feel that you completely missed raising the issue with them at a time when something might really have been wrong.

Regardless of exactly what you say, remain firm but keep an even tone. Remember that all of this will be useless if it is said in an angry, accusatory tone. You can be insistent without being upset or demanding.

"YOU'RE NOT SO GREAT YOURSELF"

Since the best defense is a good offense, you may find yourself attacked when you bring up this issue. The person may tell you that you're no judge of how someone should eat because you're too fat yourself. Or they might say that *you* diet all the time—what gives you the right to say anything? You count calories, too. You worry about your weight. Or they may accuse you of other problems—your drinking, your poor relationships, your own vices, or fears. They'll know exactly what to say to make you question yourself.

Don't get pulled in. It doesn't matter what your problems are at this moment. In fact, you might tell them that if they are worried about something you do, you two can find another time to talk about it. That is not the issue right now. You might start to feel insecure about what you're saying. "How *can* I help? I have my own problems." If you start to say this to yourself, stop! Of course, you have problems—we all do—but this doesn't mean you can't be helpful to someone else.

"YOU'RE WRONG"

The other person may simply say that you're wrong. They'll tell you that you're just panicking or that you're not living with them, so how could you know, anyway? They'll tell you everyone diets and that they are no different—or that they have a nervous stomach or gluten intolerance and that the vomiting has nothing to do with bulimia.

You must remember that it is always possible that you *are* wrong. Because you suspect a problem does not always mean that one exists. Say that you know this is a possibility and that you are prepared to be wrong. However, point out what you *have* seen, why you *are* worried. Tell them at this point that you still have questions and would like to talk about them.

NOW WHAT?

WHEN THINGS GO WELL

The other person may be able to acknowledge that they know they are having a rough time. Or they may disagree that a problem exists but they still seem willing to talk. They may start out resentful but ultimately be able to consider what you have to say. In these cases, you have gotten off to a good start.

With the problem out in the open, it is now important that you follow through with the goals of your discussion. If (such as in the case of friends) you just wanted to let the person know you're concerned, then you have already accomplished what you set out to do. Perhaps you can discuss together how you may continue to be of support. Most likely though, your goal will involve helping the person evaluate whether a problem exists or what needs to be done next. In fact, if you are concerned about a child or teenager, you will probably need to arrange for the person's treatment yourself. Chapter 6, "Seeking Help," will guide you in the steps you need to take next. Perhaps you want to speak with the person about how the eating behaviors are interfering in your life, or how you are concerned in general about your relationship with them. Chapters 7, 8, and 9 will provide guidelines for this.

At age 16, Karen lost over 20 pounds in just a couple of months. "And she was thin to begin with," her parents had told me. Karen describes her experience of being approached by her parents this way:

> I know I was eating less and less, but my stomach just wouldn't go down. I felt fat no matter what my parents said. I could hear my parents arguing about what to do. My mother wanted to leave me alone; she thought it was just a phase I was going through. My father was frightened and thought I should be forced to eat. That fight went on for a long time, and meanwhile I wasn't eating. Then one day, and I don't know how it happened, my parents together said they had to speak to me. I said I had nothing to say to them, but they said, "You don't have to say anything. Just listen."
>
> Then they said, "We love you too much to let you do this to yourself. You're wasting away. You don't go out anymore, you don't see your friends, and we're worried. We spoke to a therapist who specializes in eating issues and we made an appointment for all of us to see her." At first, I told them I wouldn't go. But neither one of them would budge. They said I had no choice. Usually when they would try to tell me what to do, I would get them off my back by listing all their faults. Sometimes I would just complain about one to the other. I tried all this, but nothing worked—so here I am.

Deborah, 32, was first confronted about her behavior by her husband:

> I'd been married two years and I was secretly eating and getting rid of the food the whole time. Before I was married,

I'd been bulimic for eight years. For two of those years I was still living with my family. I ate more food at dinner than everyone in the family combined, yet I was the thinnest.

After meals I would spend an hour throwing up in the bathroom. No one ever said anything. They would tease me about taking such long showers.

Then I got married and did the same thing, and my husband never said anything either. I really thought no one noticed.

But one day, my husband said he had to talk to me. He told me he was afraid I would be angry at him, but he said he couldn't live with himself any longer if he didn't say anything. He knew I was throwing up and he said he was scared about what that meant for him and for me. We were planning to have children and he was afraid it might interfere with my getting pregnant. He wanted me to get some help—maybe go to therapy or attend a support group—and he said he would come, too, if that would help. He told me he loved me and would do anything to help me. He was crying when he told me all this and my husband never cried. I've been so embarrassed about what I do. I always felt that no one would want me if they found out about it. My husband's support scared me. But it was the first time I really took seriously what I was doing. It was the first time I was able to face it myself.

MISSED ATTEMPTS

Bringing up your concerns will not always go well. A mother called us in tears about a confrontation she'd had with her

17-year-old daughter, Kat. She suspected her daughter was bulimic and had tried to speak to her about it:

> *I knew something was wrong with Kat. Food was disappearing from the kitchen and she never ate in front of anyone. I found empty laxative boxes in the wastebasket, and she spent much longer than anyone needs to in the bathroom. This morning I went to the bathroom. It stank from vomit. Something inside me snapped. I went into Kat's room and screamed, "What's the matter with you? Are you sick? Who does this kind of thing?" She was quiet and didn't say anything. I felt desperate to say something that would have an effect on her. The only thing I could think of to make her stop was this: I told her if she kept doing this, I'd tell all her friends. They thought she was Miss Perfect; wait until they heard this.*
>
> *She just looked at me like she could see through me and said, "Get out of my room, I hate you, I have nothing to say to you." I left the room, but now I don't know what to do next.*

This mother, out of her frustration, approached her daughter in a way that led to misunderstandings, hurt, and anger. As many of us do in difficult situations, she had let the problem go on without saying anything, hoping it would go away, until she felt overwhelmed. She approached her daughter angrily and, as a result, her daughter defended herself with silence and insults.

The mother's goal of stopping the bulimia was an impossible one—defeat was inevitable. It would have been less burdensome had she not walked in with such an overwhelming task on her hands. A more manageable goal would have been just to talk.

She also would have had a much better chance at being understood had she approached her daughter at a calmer moment. She and her daughter had a history of arguing. It may have been unrealistic to think she could have approached such a difficult issue without it ending once again in a fight. In this case, the mother needed support in handling her daughter. One way to achieve this would have been to speak with her partner before she said anything. If she felt she couldn't talk without getting upset, perhaps her partner could have approached their daughter or they might have done it together. If she were calmer, she might have been able to speak to her daughter in a more collaborative way. For example: "Kat, we know you're having problems with food. You always seem worried that you're eating too much. We've also heard you throwing up and that worries us. We want to help you with this and we want you to know we're here for you. Let's talk about what's going on."

No one ever really talks like this but it's a direction to keep in mind if you need to bring something up with someone. In this mom's case, her partner's presence might have tempered the reaction, but if that wasn't an option, it may have been helpful for her to have consulted a professional before speaking to Kat. There was no reason that she *had* to do it alone.

In another situation, Marie called us about her husband, George, whom she feared had a problem with food:

> *George has always been overweight, but that's not really the problem. I don't mind big men. It's just that in the last few years all he seems to think about is food and his weight. He goes from one diet to another but nothing*

*seems to work: Within a week or two, he's eating what-
ever he wants again.*

*The problem is that he never seems happy except for
that first day or two he's on a diet. Then he feels hopeful
and excited. But as soon as he blows it, he's back obsess-
ing about what he's eating and how heavy he is; he doesn't
want to go out; he just mopes around the apartment—
eating! Last weekend, I finally had it. We had been planning to go skiing and at the last minute (after blowing
another diet, of course) he said he was too tired to go. I
couldn't believe he was doing this again. I lost it. "You're
not too tired," I yelled. "You're too fat—you don't have the
energy to do anything except eat." He stopped speaking to
me and I don't know what to do.*

Marie, like Kat's mother, approached her husband when
she had lost control of her feelings. She was frustrated and disappointed and certainly was not in a position to be supportive. Because she was approaching George when he had let her
down, it was unclear whether Marie's goal was to do anything
but retaliate for the disappointment she had experienced. If
Marie wanted to fight with George, that was one thing. But if
she hoped to change the situation, she would need to speak to
George when she had thought through what she needed to say.

A more constructive way to approach George would have
been for Marie to say: "George, I love you, but you're so down
all the time. You're always shutting me—and everyone else—
out. I'm worried about your weight, that something will happen to you physically—but I'm also worried that we're so
distant from each other now. I miss you. I want to know how
I can help."

Think about your own situation. What do you want to say? A young patient of ours laughingly says, "Everyone should ask before they say something: *What did you* THINK *would happen?*" That's what we're asking you to do. Think carefully: Will your words have the effect you want them to have? And if not, is there anyway else to say it?

WHAT TO DO IF IT DOESN'T WORK

Bringing a problem out into the open is not always going to go smoothly. You may need to try more than once before you are able to express yourself in a way that can be heard and accepted. If so, let some time pass after your first encounter. Then broach the subject again.

In some cases, no matter what you do or say, there may be a steadfast refusal to talk or to acknowledge your concerns. When that happens, you have to decide what to do next. What you can do is the subject of the following chapter.

5.

WHEN SHE SAYS NOTHING IS WRONG

Coping with Denial

WHAT IF THE PERSON YOU CARE ABOUT REFUSES TO CONSIDER THAT a problem exists? She either denies a problem and insists nothing is wrong, or she refuses to take the problem seriously.

Whether you merely suspect a problem or know that one exists, this is inevitably a difficult situation and you are going to need help. You cannot assess the seriousness of the situation or know what to do next on your own. The assessment of an eating disorder is a complex and difficult task. Even professionals cannot always tell if a problem is part of a temporary phase or whether it signals the beginning of a full-blown eating disorder. This is certainly not something that you should expect yourself to know.

YOU DON'T NEED TO GO IT ALONE

The best way for you to proceed is to contact a professional for a consultation. The purpose of a consultation in this situation is not necessarily for starting treatment, but to receive help in deciphering the seriousness of what you are observing, and, given the complexities of your particular situation, knowing what you can do. Consultations can be anywhere from one to a few sessions.

When you go for a consultation, you should let your family member, partner, or friend know that you take the situation seriously enough to speak with someone. You should let them know what you are doing, but it is not necessary for you to have their consent. Seeking help is not just for them but also for *you*. You need to find a way of better coping with or handling a situation that is difficult for you. If treatment is in fact needed, and your intervention results in the person seeking help, therapy will be *much* more effective if the eating disorder has been in existence for a short duration. Therefore, it is critically important that you seek a consultation when you first suspect there is trouble. Even though it may be frightening or difficult to confront the person you care about, the good that may come in initiating a discussion early on far outweighs any conflict that may occur by bringing it up. *Don't* second-guess your inclination to get help—*don't* put it off or give up. A professional can always tell you if it's better to back off.

There are many types of professionals or groups you can contact to help you know how to proceed. For example, you may want to contact an eating-disorder specialist or center, a peer support group, or perhaps a hotline. If you are in a college setting, the available resources would include the college health services or a dorm counselor. In work settings, there may be employee assistance programs where counselors are available. The types of resources available are explained in Chapter 6.

Before you actually call or set up an appointment to speak with someone, it is a good idea to organize your thoughts:

- Have a clear idea of the behaviors you see that are worrisome. Look over the checklists in Chapter 1 and make a list of the various signs and symptoms you've seen.
- Think about whether there has been a worrisome change in the person's behavior or mood. Can you tell when these changes began? How long have they been going on?
- If you know of or suspect any drug or alcohol abuse, be prepared to speak about this.

  It is particularly important to report any alarming behaviors such as talk of suicide, suicidal gestures, and self-mutilating behaviors (for example, cutting). Does the sufferer complain of physical problems such as fainting, heart palpitations, or light-headedness?
- Evaluate if and how the impact of the eating behavior has been disruptive in the household. For example, is food missing? Does the person you care about refuse to eat meals with the family? And if they do, are mealtimes stressful?
- If there has been a change in your relationship, plan to talk about what this change is and how long it has been going on. (For example, are you arguing more? Does the person you care about spend less time with you?)
- Discuss what you have tried to do about the situation and what the results have been. Describe discussions or confrontations you have had and what the reactions have been.

Know that you may be asked about any family history of eating disorders, substance abuse or mental illness. It's important to be able to talk about this as well as any life changes or difficulties the family may be going through now.

PLANS OF ACTION

Depending on your situation, some plans of action may work better than others. What you are advised to do will take into account how severe the situation appears to be, the person's age, their capacity to care for themselves, and your relationship to them.

There are no clear-cut rules as to how to proceed. Each situation differs, and that is why the opinion of a professional is necessary at these times. The following are some examples of how different families, spouses, and friends were advised to act in their particular situations.

THEY JUST WON'T GO

Mr. and Mrs. Steiner's 15-year-old daughter was severely underweight but refused to acknowledge a problem or to see a therapist. This is what they were advised to do:

When Mrs. Steiner called us, her daughter, Lee, at five foot five, had already dropped from 110 pounds to 90 pounds. The Steiners had not called sooner because Lee had angrily refused to see anyone for help and kept saying that she felt fine and had things under control. The Steiners thought they would make things worse if they pushed too hard. But as Lee grew thinner and thinner and became isolated from friends, Mrs. Steiner felt they could no longer sit back.

We told Lee's mom that we knew how fierce kids could be and that we assumed Lee would be furious. But we didn't want the Steiners to look back in several years and feel they missed how much Lee was hurting (even if Lee said everything was fine). Lee could die if nothing was done. The parents were told that they had to bring Lee in for a consultation. This was not to be Lee's choice.

Mrs. Steiner feared a scene. She imagined herself and her husband literally carrying a kicking, screaming teenager into our offices. We realized this was possible, but still a better option than ignoring that their daughter was in real trouble. With our urgent support, an interesting thing happened. Lee's mom and dad were able to be forceful (verbally, not physically) with Lee, and she came into treatment—sulking, but without the tantrum we had all expected. What was clear was that in other attempts to get Lee in for a consultation, the Steiners had backed down when Lee got angry. When Lee realized her parents meant business, she yielded to their authority.

ISN'T MONEY A BRIBE?

In another situation, a parents' support group encouraged the parents of an anorexic daughter to use financial leverage as a way of bringing their daughter into treatment. There are times when withdrawal of financial support may be helpful as a means of showing that you mean business. A symptomatic daughter who is in a life-threatening situation cannot have the freedom to make her own decisions. The Robertsons are an example of how one family used the withdrawal of financial support to intervene in a potentially harmful situation.

Jenny and Lou Robertson contacted F.E.A.S.T. (https://www.feast-ed.org), an online support community for families, because they were desperate about how to handle the situation with their 24-year-old daughter Carey. Carey was planning to spend the year abroad, pursuing her career in art history by attending classes in Italy. Her acceptance to these classes was a long-awaited opportunity and the Robertsons had decided to pay Carey's expenses as a belated graduation gift. Carey had spent the previous year eagerly planning and anticipating this move. In the past three months, however, the Robertsons grew concerned that something was wrong. It seemed as if Carey had stopped eating.

Whenever the family got together, Carey refused meals, choosing to go to her room and exercise instead. She repeatedly asked her older sisters whether she looked fat. When Carey and her mother went shopping for clothes for the trip, Mrs. Robertson realized that her once-normal-weight daughter had dropped at least two clothing sizes in the last several months. In fact, at one point, they had to go to the children's department to find anything that would fit. Carey was delighted. Mrs. Robertson was horrified. She could see her daughter was not well— and she was about to leave the country for a year!

The person who spoke to the Robertsons insisted that they question why they were going to support Carey's trip to Europe when Carey was clearly in trouble. The Robertsons protested the suggestion. This was a promise they had made to their daughter. She had been planning this for a year. Wouldn't she get worse if they withdrew their support? Wouldn't she hate them for doing this?

But the advice remained firm. The Robertsons were told that they had to tell Carey that they could not pay for this trip because she was in trouble and needed help. She was not taking care of herself in the States; how would she feel alone in Europe? Carey had to see a professional who could determine whether she was healthy enough to continue plans for the trip. It might be possible that help could be set up for her in Europe.

Chances were more likely, however, that Carey would need to postpone the trip until her feet were on the ground.

The Robertsons ended up taking the advice, but dreaded the confrontation with Carey. When they spoke to Carey, they told her that they would be ignoring a serious problem if they supported the trip. They said that their financial support would be contingent upon her going for a consultation and having a professional determine whether she was healthy enough to go. Carey blew up. "You promised me," she screamed. "I can't believe you're backing out of a promise. I've been looking forward to this for a year and now you say something? If you're so worried, why didn't you say anything sooner?"

Remembering the support that the Robertsons had behind them, they held firm. They told Carey:

> *We're sorry we didn't say something earlier. We have given this a lot of thought, and we're afraid that if we go along with the trip, we will just be paying attention to the part of you who is competent and successful. But there is another part of you who doesn't have a voice, who is scared and worried and doesn't know what to do. If we let you go, we will be ignoring a big part of you. We feel horrible about this but we can't ignore that you are really troubled.*

Carey screamed that she wasn't troubled—*they* were troubled and they were certainly going to make her troubled now. She told her parents they weren't trustworthy and that they were ruining her life. Carey's remarks stung, but the Robertsons were now determined, buoyed by the support they had been given. They kept telling themselves that they weren't the only ones who thought this was the right decision. Ultimately, there was nothing Carey could do. Mrs. Robertson set up the consultation herself and both parents accompanied Carey to the meeting. The therapist agreed that Carey was in deep trouble and supported the Robertsons in postponing the financing of the trip.

Despite being upset, however, Carey started treatment.

Doing what the Robertsons did is not easy. Carey was enraged at their decision, insisting she was okay. However, if the Robertsons had backed down, they would have neglected a part of Carey that could only speak up through the weight loss—the skinny, scared little girl who felt overwhelmed by the prospect of a year in another country. By telling Carey they would not endorse or pay for the trip at this point, they were acknowledging Carey's inability to take adequate care of herself at this time.

HOW CAN I MAKE MY PARTNER CHANGE? THEY ARE NOT MY KID

If the person you are concerned about is your spouse or partner, you're not going to be able to make unilateral decisions about what happens next. Taking a firm stand about how the problem is hurting not only them but you and your relationship will usually get the person's attention and can be a first step in gaining their cooperation.

Ben, 35, describes how he approached his wife, Janet, 33, during a time when their marriage was clearly in trouble:

> For months, things seemed to be going wrong in our marriage. Janet complained I worked too much; I thought she was depressing to be around—always complaining about her weight when I thought she looked fine. I know the two of us were spending less and less time together—to

be honest, I think I was hiding out in my work. But one weekday I got a call from our friend, Liz. Liz said that every time she called Jan, she was told that it was a bad time. "Is she okay?" Liz wanted to know. "I haven't seen her in weeks and she and I used to speak every day."

Liz's call scared me. Was I missing something that was going on with Jan? When I started to pay more attention, I noticed that Janet was in the bathroom far too often, and when she wasn't in the bathroom, she'd be eating. It occurred to me that not only was Jan putting Liz off, but she wasn't in touch with anyone anymore.

I told Jan I wanted to speak with her. She had once talked about having had a history of bulimia, but she hadn't referred to it in years. This time, I told her what I'd been observing and about Liz's call. I said that I knew things weren't great between us and that I was worried that I was making her sick. I was trying to be caring and open, but she just looked at me and said, "You're not making me do anything." I wanted to know what she was going through. She said, "Nothing. Why are you suddenly so interested, anyway?" I couldn't believe she was being so cold when I was trying to reach out to her. That morning was a disaster. I started yelling at her and she cried; we ended in silence.

I guess, though, it sort of woke me up. In the afternoon I called a friend who is a therapist and spoke to her about Jan. She suggested that I try again but in a different manner.

This time I stayed firm. I told Jan that our marriage was in trouble. We could either let it die or try to do something about it. I wanted to talk about what we could

*do. I told her that for the marriage to work, I needed her
to speak to someone about her bulimia. But it wasn't all
up to her; I wanted to know what she needed from me.*

*I think that this way of talking surprised Jan. I guess
she expected more of an attack. When I told her that I
was willing to do something too, she was more willing
to talk to me. We went to see a couples' therapist. Once
we were in treatment, Jan was able to talk about how
her worries about our marriage made her want to block
everything out by eating. She acknowledged her eating
problem and began to work on it. On my part, I had to
deal with my own eagerness to retreat into work. In fact,
the therapist kept saying that my working was as much of
an addiction as Jan's eating. We both had a lot of work to
do to get our marriage back on track.*

THEY ARE MY BEST FRIEND. IF I SAY SOMETHING, THEY'LL NEVER TALK TO ME AGAIN

In some cases, particularly when friends and colleagues are involved, you will not be advised to further confront the person
you are concerned about. Instead, a professional or counselor—
or a parent—should be contacted. Laura and Jessica were in
such a situation.

Laura and Jessica were roommates at a Midwestern univer-
sity. They didn't know each other before rooming together but
by luck they got along perfectly.

When they first arrived at school and were homesick, they
could talk to each other. No matter what happened at school
or socially, whether times were exciting or disappointing, they

could handle it together. Freshman year was turning out better than either had hoped.

Then, in the second semester, Laura noticed a change in Jessica. Suddenly Jessica always had an excuse for why she wasn't coming to the dining hall. Before, they would order pizzas when they had a late study night. Now Jessica was never hungry. She didn't want late-night snacks. Laura thought Jessica's behavior was strange and she asked Jessica why she didn't seem to eat much anymore. Jessica would answer that she did eat, it was just at different times, and because Laura didn't see her didn't mean she wasn't eating.

Laura wanted to believe Jessica. She knew Jessica was losing weight, but Laura kept putting it out of her mind. One night when Jessica thought Laura was sleeping, Jessica undressed in their room instead of in the bathroom. Laura was horrified. She'd never seen anyone in the flesh who looked so thin. The only people Laura had seen that looked like that were in photographs: They were the pictures of concentration camp survivors. But no one who had access to food could look like that.

Laura didn't know what to do. The dorm counselor had lectured all the residents about anorexia. She wanted to help Jessica but knew if she told the counselor, Jessica would never speak to her again. But how could she not do anything? Then again, this could just be a phase and Jessica would start eating again. Perhaps Laura could figure out some way to help Jessica that wouldn't involve telling any of the school authorities.

Unfortunately, Jessica would hear nothing of Laura's concern. She told Laura to mind her own business. Laura was stunned. Jessica had never spoken to her like this before. "I can't stand to watch you do this to yourself," she told Jessica. "You need help. I'm going to speak to our dorm counselor."

"Speak to whomever you want," Jessica sarcastically responded.

Laura did speak to the counselor, who then insisted on speaking with Jessica. School authorities were alerted and Jessica's parents were contacted. Laura's actions resulted in Jessica's taking a year's leave from school, going into a treatment facility, and getting help.

"I hated Laura that whole year," says Jessica, now 22 and recovered from anorexia. "But now I think she saved my life."

BUT SHE'S MY MOM/HE'S MY DAD

One of the harder situations we hear about is when someone is worried about their parent. When we first wrote the book, eating disorders had not been entrenched in the culture long enough for us to hear much about kids who grew up with parents who were anorexic or bulimic. But by the time of the writing of this book, we now have generations of kids who have grown up with moms who never have had a bite of their birthday cake, dads who miss important occasions because they have to get their workout in or invariably we hear about parents who talk endlessly about being fat and losing weight.

Or another concern we hear from kids is this: "Do you know what it's like to have a really thin mom and you're the kid who is just regular weight? Every day you feel your mother's disgust when you eat or when she looks at your body. Do you know what that does to your self-esteem, even when your mom says she loves you?" Unfortunately, and not surprisingly, many of these questions come from kids who are now, as teens or young adults, in treatment themselves for disturbed body image and eating disorders.

So even if it is a parent about whom you are worried, it is okay to have an open talk about what you see, how it is affecting you, what you want your mom or dad to do. In fact, often it is with the urgency of a son or daughter's concern, not that of a spouse or partner, that we see parents coming in for help with their own eating concerns. Depending upon your age and your relationship with your parent, you may want to talk to your mom or dad privately about your concerns. Make sure to get a time when you can talk openly and honestly. But, like in other situations, be prepared for denial or minimalization of the problem. Stay steady with your concerns but if you don't feel heard or nothing changes, make sure you speak to another adult who cares about your parent. Is there someone else who could speak to your parent with you? Could this be your parent's partner, a sibling, a close relative? It's important to let someone know you are worried. Just like we tell parents, you don't want to look back and feel like you never did anything to help.

But just as important, when you are growing up with a parent in trouble, it is really important that you have someone to talk to. You need your worries to be heard and a place where your own sense of yourself can be separated from your idea of what your parent wants you to be. Sometimes the only person whom you will be able to change is you. Make sure you get the support that you need.

NO TIME TO WASTE: EMERGENCY SITUATIONS

Some situations are urgent and you will need to act immediately to ensure the well-being of the person you care about. In these cases, an immediate treatment evaluation is imperative. The situations we are referring to involve the potential of suicide, physical harm—even medical instability due to starvation.

Suicide attempts are not common but at times can occur as a result of the torment and despair associated with an eating disorder. If a suicidal gesture is made—or even if suicide is only mentioned—there is reason to consider the situation an emergency. You need to call for help at once. In these cases, it is better to overreact than do nothing.

More often when there is a struggle with bulimia, not anorexia, we sometimes see people who cut their bodies superficially without the intent of killing themselves. Cutters explain that when they hurt themselves, they are not trying to die, but that the physical pain contains and narrows the emotional pain. "When I scratch myself with a nail, suddenly everything gets quiet and all my focus goes on that one little part of my body. If I'm upset or angry, I feel like I have to do it. And then suddenly everything is calm." While cutting is not necessarily an attempt at suicide, it is nonetheless potentially dangerous and certainly a sign that someone is having a rough time. If you know someone is cutting, push them to talk to someone. They are hurting. You don't want to ignore them.

In some situations, talk of suicide (or cutting) can be a daily occurrence in which you are held hostage. Although each threat may not require an intervention, you should not evaluate this on your own: Professional assessment is needed.

The other emergency situation involves the possibility of significant medical problems or even death due to physiological damage. While death occurs less often among bulimics than anorexics, there have been cases of heart failure in both populations. Anorexia can result in many complications secondary to starvation, in particular fluid and electrolyte imbalances. Fluid imbalance means that the person is dehydrated; electrolyte imbalance refers to potassium depletion, which can cause heart failure. Unfortunately, these imbalances often occur without ongoing signs of something being wrong. Therefore, it should be considered an emergency if someone faints, collapses, or is too weak to walk. While you may know that someone is severely eating disordered by their low weight or constant vomiting, the signs of physical deterioration we have just described sometimes are the only ways of knowing that the person needs medical stabilization. Again, you must act immediately and call for help.

In these cases, you will likely be advised that immediate medical attention is required. This means that you will be told to take the person for a medical evaluation at once. Don't expect the other person to be a participant in getting help. Certainly, you want to approach them in the manner we have been describing all along. Be calm and firm. Tell the person why you are alarmed, why the situation must be taken seriously, and what you are going to do (that is, that you will take them to a doctor with expertise in eating disorders or an eating disorder facility for an evaluation). Hear the person you care about out; give them time to talk. But it's likely that this will not be a good time for a calm discussion. Anticipate that they may refuse to go; it is likely you will be met with a fight. But no matter how fierce they battle, they have no choice here. When someone is this physically debilitated or psychologically distressed, they are not in the position to be able to judge what is best. You must do *whatever* is needed to make sure they will receive immediate help.

If you are an acquaintance, roommate, or if you are not an adult yourself, you may not be in the position to assist the person on your own. If that is the case, other professionals (such as school or dorm counselors) may intervene to take care of the person in trouble. If there are no authorities or professionals available, you may need to contact the family. This is not the time to worry about politeness or confidences; someone may be in real danger.

WHEN YOU NEED TO LEAVE IT BE

In contrast to emergency situations, there are times when the best thing to do is to leave the situation alone. Eating disorders receive a lot of attention in the media and you may find yourself sensitized to and worried about an eating behavior that is not a signal of a serious problem, but part of a phase. This is not an evaluation you can make on your own but there may be times when the result of a professional or medical evaluation is that your worries are ill-founded. In this situation, if the advice is given by a professional with expertise in eating disorders, it is best to leave things alone and not pursue the matter with the other person. In these cases, pushing the issue when you've been told to leave it alone might only create a power struggle in which the other person may continue eating (or not eating) as a way of doing what *they* want to do, not what *you* want. A problem can develop where none would otherwise have existed. If you are not convinced, get a second opinion. If you are once again told not to worry, catch your breath, pull back as best you can, and know you can reevaluate the situation in a couple of months if nothing changes.

LET'S TALK ABOUT WEIGHT: CONTROVERSY ABOUNDS

If your son or daughter is eating in a way in which weight is quickly being gained, this is going to be really hard. No one wants their kid to have to face the shame and bullying that is an inevitable part of being in a large body in our culture. That being said, new research and ongoing general observation indicates that putting a kid on a diet almost never works and often results in even more weight gain once the diet is relinquished. Weight Watchers recently came out with a program aimed specifically for kids that has received extreme backlash.

Here's what you need to know: If your son or daughter is bingeing, hording food, or eating endlessly through the day and night, it is likely that indeed a problem exists. But just focusing on the food is *not* going to help. It's a time to try to talk, to find out what's on your kid's mind, to wonder with your child what would be on their mind if they weren't grabbing food. There's no question food has to be addressed but this doesn't mean putting your child on a weight-loss program.

Important rules of thumb would be to:

1. Set general and predictable times for meals.

2. Have a rule that while snacks are allowed, the amount needs to be monitored. Would you be comfortable with allowing your child two snacks or desserts a day? Your child can decide whether those snacks will be eaten during snack times or after meals. This may seem like a lot but it is certainly in

the realm of what kids normally eat and will be significantly less than what a binge would entail.

3. Make sure there are healthy foods in the home. In this regard, pay attention to how food is available throughout the day. If cake and cookies are always available, if cheese and crackers sit out on a tray throughout the day, it's not fair (and likely impossible) to assume that a child or teen struggling with eating will be able to say no.

4. Have movement or exercise be a regular (and ideally fun) part of your child's daily activities.

5. Teach your child to pay attention to what they feel inside when they reach for food. Are they physically hungry? When do they get full? If they are not hungry, what else might they need?

6. Focus on health not appearance. It isn't healthy to binge on food. And likely it doesn't feel good physically after a few minutes of eating. How your child feels is much more important than the weight itself.

7. In that spirit, importantly, focus on all the ways your child is beautiful, not just their looks. And give the message that all bodies can be beautiful.

The most important goal is that you want to encourage your son or daughter to listen to themselves, to pay attention to how food is used to cope, and to develop self-care, agency, and joy regarding one's health and well-being.

We know this is hard. Challenge yourself to question the values you have. Are you missing the beauty of your child because you want them to be someone else? These are difficult questions for everyone.

If food is being turned to as a way of coping, a therapist can help understand why this may be happening and what else someone can do to deal with feelings and complicated experiences. A dietitian can help explain the role of food, what makes for a healthy body, what choices someone can have when they want to eat. But be very careful about putting your son or daughter on a weight-loss plan. The chances are extremely high that even if weight is lost, either it will be put back on or an eating disorder will develop.

ACCEPTING YOUR LIMITATIONS

No matter what action is called for, even in the most extreme circumstances, there will always be limits to how effective you can be in influencing someone else's behavior. You may not be able to ensure that someone seeks or stays in therapy or, even if they do, that anything will change.

Shannon, the mother of 24-year-old Tamara, had spent the last 10 years grappling with Tamara's struggle with bulimia and anorexia. In the early years, when Tamara was literally starving herself, Shannon and her ex-husband spent years collaboratively in a family-based treatment, trying in any way they could to help their daughter eat. Tamara's relentless insistence to starve ultimately landed her in multiple residential and outpatient programs. The only change that Shannon saw was her daughter fluctuating from anorexia to bingeing to relentless exercise and purging. Her daughter was always in therapy (Shannon didn't even want to think how much it had cost) and at this stage of the game, she was being encouraged by Tamara's therapist to step back and let Tamara take hold of her own life, no matter what that looked like.

But the last time Tamara came home for a visit, her clothes were once again hanging on her and despite a hot summer day, Tamara kept her jacket on the entire day. Shannon hit the roof.

These kinds of situations are terrifying and maddening; you face the stark limitations of being a family member, partner, or friend. We do not know what makes people change. What we do know is that no matter how bad the situation is, without support, it could be worse. We've seen situations in which recovery hasn't happened for many, many years. Then, for reasons no one can really explain, the person decides that they have had it with the torture of the disorder and they start to eat. Health, for the first time in years, is suddenly possible. No matter what you—or a professional—does, the other person is not going to allow for change until they are capable of accepting the seriousness of the matter themselves. And most daunting for some, genetic and physiological predeterminants that we don't yet understand may keep them from ever being able to stop food restriction. No matter what the psychological picture, change doesn't occur.

When you are faced with this kind of helplessness, you absolutely must speak to someone else—not about the person in trouble, but about yourself and what has happened to your life. This is why this book was written. There are things you can do, but often, and sometimes more importantly, sometimes there are things you can't do—and one of the goals of this book is to help you recognize that. When you can't save your child, your partner, or your friend, the feelings that ensue are bound to be overwhelming—and you can't go it alone.

In most cases, there are steps you are able to take to help someone turn in the right direction and change their life. Chapters 7, 8, and 9 are devoted to discussing the process of recovery—your recovery as well as that of the person you love. Even in the worst of situations, there are many things you can do to allow for communication, connection, and understanding. The ongoing goal is to create the best possibility for recovery—recovery for your loved one, recovery for your relationship, and recovery for your own well-being.

6.

NO ONE CAN GO IT ALONE

Seeking Help

IT HAS NOW BEEN WELL OVER 40 YEARS SINCE EATING DISORDERS FIRST emerged as a significant problem in our culture. Treatments have developed, evolved, and changed as a result of learning more about what is needed both psychologically and physiologically. Initially, we were excited and hopeful that we could develop a treatment protocol that would stop these disorders in their tracks. We have made significant progress in allowing for change and many directions have emerged as potential answers. But questions loom. In the most extreme situations, we still don't have a clear-cut path for recovery. Often the question most asked is not if treatment is available but what should that treatment be? What can best allow for recovery? How intensive should care be established? And most pertinently now, how families can best be of help?

PLANNING FOR THE PERSON IN TROUBLE

When someone who is eating disordered is in need of services, they should be seen for a consultation with a professional who can help outline the type of treatment approach that would be most beneficial. Even at this first juncture, questions arise.

Should the initial evaluation be done by a physician who can assess physical damage, or a therapist with expertise in assessing the psychological reasons for the problem at hand? And what about medication or an evaluation by a nutritionist? The varied physiological complications that result from disturbed eating behaviors may require the attention of a myriad of specialists, including internists, dentists, gynecologists, and dieticians.

No matter what issue you are facing, you cannot assume that an eating disorder is being comprehensively treated unless a physician who specializes in eating disorders is involved to assess the potential damages secondary to the eating disturbance. Medical assessment and stabilization are always the first line of treatment with any eating disorder. Unattended physical complications in all eating disorders can lead to serious health problems and, in the worst case, death. In particular, the treatment of anorexia must always involve the ongoing active presence of a physician who will monitor health and weight and who will, most often, determine whether a higher level of treatment, such as residential care, is needed.

The person seeking help should be encouraged to be open and frank about their eating behaviors. One young woman who binged and vomited daily told us that she went to an internist because she was concerned about the enlarged glands in her throat. While swollen glands are a very common side effect of purging, this person told us that she was examined and tested for Hodgkin's disease before she was able to muster the courage to admit how much she was throwing up. The internist had not had expertise with eating disorders and missed this signal of trouble. The woman, so embarrassed about the bulimia, was almost willing to be treated for cancer before she could consider revealing her problem.

If both the physician and patient are open about issues such as bingeing, vomiting, laxative abuse, and starvation, the whole assessment will be much more productive.

While a physician can determine whether treatment is needed, the actual kind of treatment pursued can take a myriad of forms. In terms of understanding what treatment is available and what medical complications need to be assessed, we have found several guides to be invaluable. At this time, *Sick Enough* by Dr. Jennifer Gaudiani is the most engaging and thorough book we can recommend regarding the medical aspects of eating disorders. The *Gürze-Salucore Eating Disorders Resource Catalogue* is an extensive resource providing books, podcasts, and a significant array of information regarding treatment and support. The Recovery Roadmap Specialists (https://www.recoveryroadmaps .com) help families find and create support structures, no matter the needed level of treatment. And take a look at Feast-ed.org, the online global community website for parents. There, an invaluable series of online booklets are offered that discuss treatment options and medical and nutritional issues.

Read anything you can. The more you know and understand, the more you can be of support in whatever treatment directions are next needed.

WHEN A PROBLEM DOES EXIST: THE FIRST LINE OF TREATMENT FOR ANOREXIA NERVOSA

If it is determined that a problem does exist, most particularly with anorexia, the first goal of treatment is medical stabilization.

This always means direct focus on food and weight. Just talking about one's feelings and experiences in and of itself will not change the restriction.

In recent years, families have been engaged to be on the front line regarding treatment intervention. That means that if you are the parent of someone who has been diagnosed with anorexia, you will have an extremely important role to play. The following section focuses on the specific role of parents or significant caretakers in the treatment of anorexia. If you are a spouse, partner, friend, or other family member, your role is going to be different than if you are the primary caretaker of someone. For now, we are focusing on parents. If you are not in this role, see the following chapters for the support and guidance you may need.

FAMILY INVOLVEMENT AND INTERVENTION

Currently, one of the most important questions is how—not if—parents should be involved in treatment. Should they actually be re-feeding their starving child or not? A treatment protocol initially termed the Maudsley approach (named after the London hospital where British researchers developed this program) urgently advocates parental involvement in the re-feeding and care of one's child or teenager with an eating disorder. With this treatment model, now more familiarly called family-based treatment (or FBT), parents are guided to re-feed their starving child. This means direct intervention at meals, with slow and gentle insistence that food is eaten over several weeks until weight is restored. Then parents are guided to relinquish control over the eating and to support more independence both with food and in other age-appropriate areas of one's life.[1]

If you have a child or teen who is clearly eating disordered, it is very likely that you have already tried to change their eating and distorted thoughts about body and food intake. You have probably reasoned with them, thought of award systems and bribes. You've tried to be encouraging. You've certainly lost your temper. All of this is normal. If these interactions with your son or daughter are working and the eating is significantly changing, you may be on the right track. Just make sure to pay attention and remember that these problems are not just about food. If the hidden parts to the disorder are not addressed, it is likely that problems will soon reemerge.

It is possible, however, that your efforts to help re-feed your child or control their bingeing episodes have not gone smoothly. This is why we have written this book. Taking control of your son's or daughter's food intake sometimes is not the best solution, even in the case of anorexia. The decision as to whether or not you should be involved in the direct feeding of your child is usually one that should not be made alone. A well-trained professional comfortable with family-based treatment can assess whether feeding interventions will help or not. Merely trying to get your son or daughter to eat is *not* family-based treatment and sometimes does not work. Control battles in some cases can make the situation worse. When feeding is undertaken within the context of family-based treatment, the goal is not merely to have your child gain weight, but to re-structure the family system. The goal is to put you as parents back in charge, united in your position regarding your child's eating. Although the process begins with your taking control, in the long run it helps you to separate from your child, paving the way for them to grow up.

Tayja and Jack had watched helplessly as their 14-year-old

daughter Kristen's weight plummeted 18 pounds over the course of just a couple of months. No matter what Tayja and Jack did, Kristen's weight continued to drop. Kristen had been taken to meet with both a therapist and physician when her parents recognized the weight loss, but nothing anyone did seemed to help and Kristen's weight kept going down. The next year Kristen spent in and out of residential care. Each time, soon after landing home from treatment, the downward weight trend would start again.

Finally, Kristen's parents decided to take things into their own hands. They had been reading about the FBT approach and decided to seek out a therapist who would help the family work in this way. They decided to dedicate as much time as was needed to getting Kristen steady again. This was no minor task. Kristen was home from school and residential programs at this point. Tayja put her job on hold and Jack minimized any outside involvements he had previously had, separate from his job. Their 16-year-old son would be away at camp, so they had the summer to dedicate to the task of getting Kristen well.

Every day, Tayja sat with Kristen for at least two hours each meal. Meal plans had been set up by the nutritionist, and Tayja and Jack insisted on the amounts that needed to be eaten. Kristen was sullen, angry, and determined not to gain weight. But her parents were equally determined and wouldn't budge. Tayja did most of the actual work, sitting with Kristen, cajoling, pushing, and making it clear that Kristen couldn't do anything else but finish her meal. Sometimes while eating they would watch TV or listen to music—there could be distractions, but Kristen had to eat. Jack supported Tayja and took over with the feeding when she felt too frustrated to continue. Slowly, Kristen got into a routine regarding the eating. She still needed to know the calories of anything she put in her mouth, and meals were still long ordeals, but by the end of the summer, Kristen had gained 10 pounds and, while work was still needed, was healthy enough to go back to school instead of going back to a hospital.

It is not clear which families benefit from FBT and which do not. As a general rule, families in which there is a significant degree of overt hostility or criticism usually do not do well with this method.[2] But each family differs—even families who function well together and who have the best of intentions, can be thwarted.

The Simons came to us for help with their 15-year-old anorexic daughter Lisa. Their daughter had lost weight more slowly than Kristen had, but over the year, Lisa had quietly given up sugar, then flour, then carbs, and their once healthy-looking daughter was now putting on clothes that fit her 10-year-old sister. The family doctor insisted that Lisa was in trouble. Quickly, the Simons began to work with Lisa's physician, a nutritionist, and a family therapist to help get Lisa back on her feet. No one, including Lisa, wanted her to leave school and get more intensive treatment.

"It's just been hell," Lisa's dad reported during a family consultation that was set up to consider what else could be done:

> My wife Debbie and I have been doing all the right things. We were patient, we'd sit with Lisa, we told her she had to eat, and we'd be at her side. But she'd sit there and have the worst look on her face, scramble her food around on her plate, and just not eat. Debbie sometimes would sit with Lisa for three hours and still nothing would happen.

I kept holding in my frustration and anger and would stay steady and calm—or just leave the room for a break. I don't know how Debbie would just sit there. But one Saturday we were trying to get out of the house to actually do something fun and the whole thing was getting delayed, maybe even canceled—and I finally just lost it. I started screaming that Lisa was ruining our family and that she might as well be in a hospital so that things could get back to normal. Debbie started to cry and scream herself, saying that I was ruining the program. Lisa just ran out of the room. We're just not sure this is something we can do. We don't know how other families do it.

Lisa's parents were very smart, sophisticated, and well intentioned. It was unclear why their work with their daughter was having no effect. They were thoughtful, working closely with a therapist, and questioning themselves at every turn. They wondered if they were doing something that they weren't aware of that was undermining their efforts. Mr. Simon wondered if Mrs. Simon was too involved with the whole eating process. She thought he was too involved with his work and not home enough, even though he felt he was. In truth, it's unclear what happened in this family. Every family has ways of interacting that aren't perfect. We just don't know enough yet to be able to say what makes one situation successful and another so difficult. Lisa did end up being admitted to residential treatment and spent the next year struggling to make changes in her life and her weight. Even though the residential program was in the picture, both Lisa and her parents used family sessions in the program to question what else needed to change in the family to better allow the process of recovery—not just for Lisa, but for her parents as well.

Some families have told us that while FBT has indeed allowed for weight stabilization, they remain stuck. "I would never allow my son to go off to camp this summer," said Donna, the mother of a 14-year-old who was now weight-restored as a result of six months of parental intervention and direct feeding. "Truth is, if I'm not there monitoring Nick, I know he will just not eat. I feel like a failure of a mom."

Indeed, for some families, a different approach to the family's involvement may be warranted. Parents may need help and exploration understanding why setting limits is so hard or how to deal with a son or daughter who just won't move forward. In these cases, the focus is on family communication and connection in addition to the needed food and weight interventions. Relational dynamics are explored and understood, parental authority is still supported, but the actual feeding is left in the hands of the therapists, food coaches, and professionals. This treatment plan still very much involves the family but takes the re-feeding out of the hands of the parents and allows for other means of both authority and support to be set up by the parents as part of the treatment protocol.

THE RELATIONSHIP MODEL: PARENTS AS PARTNERS

An alternative approach to engaging parents in the treatment of their anorexic child is a protocol we term the *Relationship Model: Parents as Partners.* Here, parents are very much a part of the treatment team but their role is not that of directly feeding their child.

The focus in this approach is similar to family-based treatment in that the authority of the parents is reinstated. And like in FBT, there is a clear path of consequences for noncompliance regarding the work toward medical stability and health.

The treatment protocol starts with an assessment by a physician knowledgeable about eating disorders. If outpatient treatment is recommended (that is, the person doesn't need immediate medical stabilization in a residential or hospital facility), a treatment team is set up with a therapist, physician, and dietician, with a weight gain goal of approximately one to two pounds weekly. A physician or dietician assesses the weight weekly and if the recommended weight is not gained, direct and immediate consequences are put into play (i.e., a valued activity such as dance or sports, will be taken away; a trip is cancelled; exercise is stopped. Or indeed a higher level of care is initiated).

The work of the parents is not to actually feed their child, but to set up and enforce clear and realistic consequences if weekly goals are not met. Physicians, therapists, dieticians, the parents, and sometimes even the school all work together to set a treatment plan in which weight goals are set and consequences are delineated at each step of the way.

A plan for more intensive treatment is immediately considered as a consequence if the person is not able to do the needed work regarding food and weight. Here it is critical that parents look into programs, see what their insurance will cover and what facilities would be realistic logistically and practically if indeed a higher level of care is needed. We often see that if a son or daughter senses that the parents would never do this, all parental authority is lost. We have also seen situations in which kids stagnate literally until the day they realize a residential program has been called and a bed is waiting for them. Within a day, restriction decreases and weight is gained.

The point here is not that of punishment or even control. The point is to assess how you as parents can maintain a position of gentle but clear authority and how your child or teen can best be guided to envision their life as their own. Thus, even if options are limited (i.e., they have to eat breakfast or they will need to go to an intensive outpatient program, as an extreme but not unfamiliar example), it still becomes their choice as to what they will do next. Parents are intensely involved in the treatment process, even if direct refeeding is not encouraged.

Rosie was 16 when she came to treatment for anorexia. In the six months leading up to her entry into treatment, she had lost almost 18 pounds, bringing her appearance from that of a toned athlete to that of an emaciated victim of starvation. Despite the rapid weight loss, she remained a straight-A student, captain of the high school basketball team (a coveted position given her young age), and was engaged with friends and a boyfriend.

Attempts by her parents to get her to eat had been complicated by the fact that both parents had highly demanding jobs that were not easy to leave and that two younger siblings had begun to leave each heated, control-battled meal crying.

We set up a plan in which Rosie was to meet with a physician (an expert in eating disorders) who determined a goal weight for her, a weight that would need to be reached if Rosie was to avoid a higher level of care, such as residential treatment. She met with a dietician who spelled out a food plan that allowed for three meals daily, two snacks, and the goal of a one-to-two-pound weight gain weekly. The work of the therapist was to meet both with Rosie individually and to include the parents in weekly updates and family sessions throughout.

The plan was set with the consequences being pretty extreme as far as Rosie was concerned. She was to follow the food plan starting right away. If she didn't comply—or if somehow weight didn't start to inch up immediately, she couldn't go to basketball that week (even though the team was now a top-ranked team gearing up for finals). And certainly, if weight didn't continue to increase, intensive outpatient programs or even residential care was to be the next step—which, as Rosie put it, "would ruin everything," basketball being the least of it.

Rosie was furious, and her parents were scared. Maybe this was just a phase; maybe she would be too overwhelmed with all on her plate to be able to gain that much weight that fast. The therapeutic work with the parents was to support them in keeping to the limit setting, to have them definitely look into programs that allowed for a higher level of care (to keep that option real), to stay close in touch with the team and explore with the therapist what was difficult for each of them regarding keeping to the plan.

There were many fears, indeed! The first week, Rosie cut corners where ever she could. At the first weigh-in, Rosie lost a half of a pound. That meant that Rosie would have three or four days—not a full week—to regain that half pound—and then another weigh-in at the end of the week to complete the ongoing goal of a pound a week. By the next week, she needed to gain yet another pound. The plan was detailed and specific—and maddening to Rosie. If she couldn't gain the two pounds in the two weeks, she would not be allowed to go to basketball practice, despite the importance of her place on the team.

Rosie was sure the added food was making her sluggish and sick. Her parents worried that it was interfering with her doing her schoolwork and performing on the team. Rosie was suddenly intolerably depressed and angry. What made it hard for Rosie's parents is that they began to think that maybe they were making things worse.

The therapist worked closely with Rosie's parents to support them in keeping to the set goals and consequences and to make sure Rosie attended all appointments. At this stage, there was little room for Rosie to do any exploration regarding what the anorexic food restriction meant to her. No insight was going to help at this stage of the game. Rosie just needed to kick and scream—and eat. But with the parents, important work was already set into play. It was clear that whenever Rosie screamed, Rosie's mom, Alicia, felt like she was suddenly back with her own tyrannical mom. The only way to avoid Alicia's mother's rages had been to always back down and comply with what was needed. If she didn't comply, Alicia was made to feel like she had done something really wrong and was a bad kid. As a result, standing up to Rosie's rages was really hard for her. When Rosie screamed that her mother was insensitive and not paying attention, it struck a chord, heightening Alicia's fear that she would lose Rosie like she ultimately lost her own mother, who no longer spoke to her. Rosie's dad, Felix, had one way of getting through tough situations: to withdraw. Thus when he was needed to stay steady with the limits, to support his wife, and to hear Rosie scream—all he wanted to do was get out of there.

With an understanding both of their backgrounds, why they were so afraid to stay steady, and the kind of support they each needed, Alicia and Felix were more easily able to be clear about consequences. They realized that they were helping their fierce but scared daughter.

Rosie definitely tested their limits. Weight jaggedly went up and down. But Alicia and Felix were able to make it clear they meant business. That first week of treatment, Rosie did not gain the needed one pound. Rosie's parents kept to the agreed limits and told Rosie that the next week of basketball was off the table. Interestingly, not only did Alicia and Felix have to face the rage of their daughter, but they also had to deal with the rage of the coach, who was losing his key player in a critical playoff week. That meant the therapist needed to speak directly to the coach and help him understand why his support was critical here. He listened and everyone held firm.

Whether it was fury or shame that allowed Rosie to use this as a turning point, whatever the motivation was, that week was the start of Rosie's continual weight gain until she reached her goal weight. She went back on the team, they won, and in one of the moments that allows all of us to see that treatment really can help, she stayed on the path to recovery over the next years.

While medical stability and symptom abatement no question are the primary goals, family interactions can be assessed and changed, even at this early stage of intervention. Overall, the goal is not merely weight gain. The work is to be interested in the family system as a whole, including what works, what doesn't, and what is needed to allow for the best route to recovery. Here communication, connection, boundaries, and limit setting are all part of the critical mix of how change can occur.

IS THE TREATMENT OF ARFID THE SAME AS THE TREATMENT OF ANOREXIA?

In many ways, ARFID has a similar presentation to anorexia. Food restriction and consequent weight loss can result in maddening family meals, with loved ones facing frustration and bewilderment as to why their child won't eat. Medical instability or growth abatement often are part of the picture. But the fear presented with ARFID is not that of getting fat but a terror of stomach pains, bloating, vomiting (which in some cases really does occur after eating, usually due to the anxiety about eating), or just a fear of the food itself.

At the time of the writing of this book, ARFID is still a fairly newly diagnosed disorder and there have not been large-scale studies as to the best modalities for its treatment. However, usually behavioral interventions are the first line of help. For young children who significantly restrict their food intake, this might mean that systematic desensitization is initially introduced. Here, the child is exposed repeatedly to new foods through play without the expectation that they actually have to eat anything. Alternately, another approach is operant conditioning in which rewards for eating certain foods are given by the therapist or caregiver.

However, not unlike the treatment of anorexia, the treatment of ARFID involves a critical question as to what the role of parents and caretakers should be. The question is not *if* the parents should be involved, but *how*.

If you are with the parent or caregiver of a child who won't eat, the question will be whether a better recommendation is a family-based treatment in which you are the one who is guided to directly re-feed your child, or the Relationship Model in which you work with a team and enforce weekly weight-gain goals, but the child is in control of what choice is made. In either case, rewards and consequences for weight gained or loss are an active part of treatment, with a higher level of care sometimes having to be the consequence if weight is not gained. No question, with young children, parental re-feeding is going to be the recommended direction to go in. But with older children and certainly with teens, the question becomes murkier. Is the best bet for you as primary caretaker to insist on eating or would it make more sense for a team to set the weight goals and for you to set the terms of enforcement?

Please refer back to the information on the treatment of anorexia to consider the issues involved in deciding how you as parents can best be involved in the treatment of your child. The balance between setting limits and supporting your child is hard for everyone, no matter the age of the child, no matter the issue. This is difficult for all of us as parents. Always there is the question as to whether you are making things better or worse, whether you really are helping your child, whether this battle is worth it. When you have a child in psychological or medical trouble, the stakes are even higher. Understanding what limit setting means to you, where you and your partner differ when it comes to caretaking, where it gets hard and why, and how to best move forward are concerns that need to be considered. What questions, other than those regarding food, need to be asked of everyone in the family to best allow recovery to move forward?

WHAT IF THE PERSON I CARE ABOUT IS EATING TOO MUCH, NOT TOO LITTLE?

HOW CAN I BE OF HELP?

While eating disorders other than anorexia and ARFID certainly involve food and weight concerns, the treatment goals of these other disorders are much less clear-cut. No question, symptom abatement must be primary. But the focus as well needs to be on what purpose the bingeing, purging, exercise, or body focus has for the person involved. Most often you won't be able to see changes in the bingeing or purging behavior right away. Often what is needed first is a growing ability to care for one's self in ways other than turning to food or body thoughts. And that is hard to put a time limit on.

In the Relationship Model, treatment often begins with a detailed assessment of when and how the problematic eating behaviors or thoughts occur. We want to know what the person likes about the way they eat now. This is often a startling question because most people enter treatment to change or get rid of the way they are eating. But when we dig closely, we hear things like "When I let go and binge, I can stop being so perfect. I actually feel like I'm relaxing for the first time all day" or "When I only eat salads or protein, I feel in control. Sort of like nothing can touch me" or "Once I purge, I feel I can start all over again.

I feel like I can start again to have a good day." Interestingly, the eating disorder has as much to do with one's identity as it has to do with food itself.

The point here is that we are trying to understand what purpose the eating behavior serves. Even when there are potential physiological causes, these behaviors can be a way of coping, a medication of sorts, that differs for each person involved. With this understanding, we try to find what else may be needed during those times. In fact, we ask each person to think of the difficult times and to imagine five things they could do instead in an attempt to address what is really needed during times they turn to disordered thoughts or behaviors. What are they feeling? Do they need to quiet themselves down? If so, how do they soothe themselves? And what about people? Why is food easier to turn to than their partner, parent, or friend? What about food itself? Is someone even hungry at these times—do they actually need to eat something? Do they even know?

Recovery is not only going to be about changing the eating disorder itself. What is needed is a better understanding of who the person is when they are bingeing or purging, or what part of the person is calling out for help at that moment. There are so many different parts to all of us. Someone can be a really responsible parent, a successful student, or a driven career person. But, for all of us, some parts of who we are may be more hidden, scared, vulnerable, or insecure.

Thus for both you as a loved one or friend, as well as for the person struggling with food and weight, the work is to get to know who is turning to the food, who is restricting, who is going out for a 10-mile run even though it's time to eat dinner with the family. Treatment thus should involve both an attempt at behavior change but also an exploration of what might better be needed at those times. The best treatment will be one that focuses both on behavior change but also on getting to know who the person is and what purpose the food or body focus serves in their life.

Where do you come in as a parent, loved one, friend, or partner? If someone you care about is suffering with bulimia, binge eating, or complicated combinations of bingeing, purging, exercising, and starving—but if medically they are not in trouble (yes, it's possible to vomit and go up and down the scale and still somehow be medically okay), your role is going to be much more complicated. While there may need to be a focus on food and possible direct interventions (see page 139), more likely your role is going to be more multi-determined, with a focus as much on who the person is as there is a focus on behaviors. Trying to help someone stop bingeing is actually harder than trying to help someone gain weight.

In these situations, the most important goal is to do what you can to set the stage for the person to develop agency and take hold of their own life in all arenas, but of course specifically with regard to food. How can you encourage them to know what they feel and what they need—other than food? If food and body obsession weren't in the picture, what would they need, both from themselves and from you?

The work when someone is medically stable but still struggling with eating and body issues is to take the time to understand how communication, boundaries, independence, and self-care are balanced in your life, in the life of the person you care about, and, of course, in the relationship itself. This is work that certainly you can do on your own but often speaking with a professional about what changes are needed can allow for these questions and open doors.

CHOOSING A THERAPIST

When someone is stuck regarding problematic eating behaviors or when your relationship with this person keeps hitting the same roadblocks, speaking to a therapist who has expertise in the treatment of eating disorders may well be needed.

If you are helping someone look for a therapist or choosing one for yourself or family, the process of a consultation is the best one we know of to evaluate a particular therapist. There are certain questions that are useful for people entering therapy to ask at the outset. As a parent arranging therapy for a minor, you may be in the position of asking these questions yourself, either on the phone, online, or during a consultation with the therapist.

QUESTIONS FOR ALL THERAPISTS

1. Ask about credentials.

   Choose a qualified practitioner who is licensed or in a licensed professional group in their respective discipline.

2. Ask about the therapist's experience and views about treatment.

   A specialization in the area of eating disorders is very important. You want to be sure the therapist has a compassionate view of the symptom and that they know that the eating behavior is related to attempts at coping with inner emotional difficulties. You will want someone who will work specifically with changing the symptom while at the same time developing an understanding of why the symptom may be needed in one's life.

If the person or family entering therapy has addictions other than food (that is, alcoholism or drug abuse), you will want to make sure that the professional is knowledgeable about and experienced in the area of addictions, is informed about and supportive of Alcoholics Anonymous or similar support networks, and is capable of dealing directly with these other addictions in addition to the eating disorder.

3. Find out how much treatment will cost.

You will find a vast range in fees depending upon the type of services being sought.

4. Inquire as to billing procedures.

Is payment required each session or once a month?

5. Find out the policy on missed sessions.

Many therapists charge for missed sessions. Can these appointments be rescheduled? Is the patient charged for vacations? In particular, if you are a parent paying for your child's individual or group therapy, will you be informed if they miss sessions? Parents and therapists have different preferences in this regard. Be sure you understand the policy before your son or daughter begins therapy so there won't be misunderstandings later on.

6. Find out about insurance reimbursement.

Depending upon your insurance plan, treatment may be partially reimbursed. Check your policy to see what coverage is possible. Also note that not all professionals take insurance reimbursement as direct payment for services.

Make sure you understand the terms of the insurance coverage, whether services for a therapist out of network will be covered, and at what point reimbursement might be terminated.

7. Find out the policy on family members' involvement.

Most importantly, particularly with adolescents and even with young adults who are supported financially, make sure you will somehow be involved in the treatment. If you are not involved directly with re-feeding your child, there are many other ways that you should be included. Parents should have a way of being involved and informed at each step of the way. Often you will be the one feeding your child. What role will you have regarding the food itself? How will you know if treatment is stalled? Will the therapist be willing to see you if you have questions or concerns?

Find out how you will be expected to be involved and what you should do if you have questions.

8. Discuss what will happen in a crisis.

If you're arranging treatment for someone else, you might want to know how the therapist handles a crisis situation. There are some situations in which you *must* be contacted by the therapist. For example, if the client is suicidal, and a minor, parents should be alerted; in the case of a married client, the partner should be called. There are some situations, however, that are more ambiguous. What if your 19-year-old daughter is taking drugs? What if an adolescent is pregnant? If you are the parents of a minor, you have a right to be contacted in certain types of situations in which your child may be in trouble. If you are a parent of someone older, or a husband or friend, your rights are less clear (even if you are paying for the therapy). At the start of therapy, discuss with the therapist how crises are handled and in what type of situations (if any) you will be contacted.

There are other questions that may be useful depending upon the type of therapy pursued.

EVALUATING THE THERAPIST

One question that is frequently asked of all types of therapists is whether it is beneficial to have a therapist who has been eating disordered. This is not necessary. What is most import-ant is for the therapist to have the empathy to feel for and un-derstand the patient's experience. Health care professionals do not need to have experienced myriad emotional problems from anxiety to depression to phobias to be helpful in treating these disturbances. Indeed, it would be impossible to have experi-enced everything that one treats.

That said, a therapist who has recovered from an eating disorder certainly can be a beacon of hope, reminding some-one that change is possible. They may also have specific tools to share that helped them through the process of recovery. But because someone has been eating disordered does not guaran-tee that they will be more understanding of the patient's ex-perience. Sometimes a therapist is still so close to their own personal struggle with food that the therapist insists on seeing the patient's difficulties as similar to their own. In any therapeutic situation, it is important that the therapist be free to understand the patient's own unique personal experience and not color it by thinking it similar to what they have gone through.

Regardless of whether a therapist is or is not eating disordered, it is also not a given that they will tell you. Ask any question you'd like at the outset. How you feel about how the question is handled, regardless of the specific answer, will be the best determination of whether the therapist will be a good fit for you or your child.

What you or the patient *should* be concerned with is the therapist's training in the area of eating disorders, experience with patients, and sensitivity to people. These are perhaps the most valuable qualities to look for in a therapist. Most important, a patient needs to feel they can trust the therapist and it feels like a good match. It is, after all, going to be a long and hard journey together; the more comfortable they are at the outset, the more likely they will be able to stick with it during the more difficult moments of treatment and thus the more effective the therapy will be.

But in your search, don't minimize the reality of finances. Sometimes in an attempt to get the "best" treatment, families or patients meet with someone they can't afford, hoping that the therapist's experience will result in a shorter length of treatment. While there is no minimizing the importance of a therapist's expertise, even with the most seasoned therapists, treatment can be a long and complicated process. Only enter into a situation that you can afford ongoing for an unspecified period of time. Otherwise the pressure for the treatment to "work" and be finished can actually thwart the work that needs to be done.

WHEN IT'S A POOR MATCH

It is not uncommon for a patient to feel unsure about a therapist in the beginning of treatment. The new patient doesn't know much about the therapist and needs time to build trust. But sometimes the relationship just may not be a good match. All too often, patients assume that discomfort about therapy is part of *their* problem. Feelings of discomfort or mistrust should not be negated. One's own intuition can be a useful resource and should be respected.

Sometimes it helps to set up a second appointment in which the patient can tell the therapist about what felt off. Sometimes voicing these apprehensions allows for a discussion that can abate the discomfort. If this doesn't happen, however, and mistrust or uneasiness continue, a consultation with someone else is in order.

The person in therapy needs to know that it is okay to leave. The therapist should be told what is wrong and why it makes sense to move on. Some therapists may want to meet one or more additional times to see if anything can be changed or to have a chance to end the relationship comfortably. This is common practice. But if the person in therapy is unhappy, endings should not drag on.

WHAT TO EXPECT FROM TREATMENT

HOW LONG WILL IT TAKE?

If someone begins the process of outpatient therapy and finds a therapist they like, this is often the start of a long process toward recovery. The most frequent question we are asked is, "How long will it take?" Unfortunately, this is also one of the hardest to answer. The time it takes depends upon many factors.

The duration of the eating disorder will certainly be a determining factor: The shorter its history, the more likely and more quickly recovery is possible. A 14-year-old who has been bulimic for under a year is more likely to benefit from therapy than a 30-year-old who has been bulimic for 15 years. This does *not* mean that therapy will be ineffective for the 30-year-old, but it will most likely take longer before an abatement in the symptoms is seen.

The severity of the problem is also a big factor. Some people, for example, vomit once or twice a week after having a big meal. Others spend most of their waking hours eating and getting rid of food. For this latter group, the eating disorder is a much more active part of one's daily life and is likely (as harmful as it is) the main way the person has to cope with feelings. In these situations, it will obviously take a much longer time. As we told a 28-year-old who was in treatment for daily body obsession, bulimia, and restriction that had begun when she was a teenager, she had literally spent *half* of her life using food, weight, and body thoughts to organize her sense of self. After a year, when she had stopped throwing up but was still afraid to eat without a strict no-carb, no-fat diet, the work was to help her understand why knowing what she wanted without an outside plan was so hard and frightening to achieve.

Other addictions, such as drug or alcohol dependency, other psychological problems, or difficulties in the family (such as substance abuse, incest, or domestic problems) will also add to the complications and therefore the length of therapy.

Change takes time. An entrenched eating disorder is a very

serious condition and treatment typically involves years, not months. Some people expect that when the eating disturbance goes away, psychotherapy is over. This is not true. The process of psychotherapy helps a person resolve the emotional dilemmas that led them to food in the first place. This process often only fully begins when the eating itself is less of an issue. When someone is in treatment, they need to develop their own pace of recovery.

WHAT BEHAVIOR CHANGES CAN YOU EXPECT TO SEE?

When someone enters treatment, the first goal has to be medical stabilization. Thus the treatment goals and picture will look very different for the starving anorexic than that of someone who is medically healthy but emotionally trapped in a cycle of bingeing and vomiting. While the main goal of treatment is always to change the disordered eating and thinking, how and when these changes occur will be evaluated differently depending upon the actual eating disorder and the severity of the problem.

For example, if someone has a long history of binge eating or bulimic behavior, the eating disorder may not abate in a predictable manner. Sometimes, the bingeing or purging actually increases at first in a last-ditch attempt to hold onto the behavior before someone has to give it up. In other situations, self-destructive eating patterns stop immediately only to begin again once the person starts to feel emotions they have kept hidden for years. In yet other situations, the bingeing or purging can fluctuate on and off for years before there is lasting change.

With bulimia or binge eating, the benefits of therapy cannot solely be measured on the basis of changes in the eating disorder itself. Sometimes quick improvements in the eating patterns are short-lived, prompted by a display of white-knuckle will-power or a wish to please the therapist. Developing a trusting relationship, being able to acknowledge and express feelings, and increasing one's self compassion and self-esteem have to be established before a more sustained change in the eating can occur. These less-observable changes are crucial as a basis of lasting change and long-term growth.

With someone who is restricting food and medically com-promised, however, the initial goals of treatment are much dif-ferent. Here, because of the potentially life-threatening aspects of anorexia or medical compromises due to ARFID, change in eating and weight need to be seen much more quickly. Some-one struggling with these disorders needs to be monitored by a physician (and often a dietician), assessed by a therapist, and weighed weekly regardless of how the family is involved. Here, one can expect that an increase in eating and weight should occur soon after treatment is initiated in order for outpatient treatment to continue. The rule of thumb is usually that a one-to-two-pound weight gain per week is needed until a goal weight is reached. If weight isn't gained within two to three weeks, the need for a higher level of care must be assessed.

Regardless of whether parents are actively engaged in re-feeding their son or daughter, they certainly need to be in-formed on an ongoing basis about how treatment is progressing and whether weight is being gained. Sometimes the therapist, doctor, and patient agree that the patient shouldn't know the actual weight itself. The number can be frightening or humil-iating and can undermine the progress. If the patient doesn't know the weight, parents shouldn't know either. That kind of secret can be too burdensome for caretakers to hold. As a result, it is not uncommon for the patient not to be informed of their actual weight and to be weighed blind, with their back to the scale. But everyone involved, parents included, do need to know whether the patient's weight is increasing, decreasing, or staying the same.

If the eating has not changed and weight is not at least steadied in the first couple of weeks, treatment assessment is needed by the entire team. If this is not done, you as parents must intervene and assess what is needed next. In this case, the first order of business is to speak with the therapist directly and see if there is a clear plan of action as to how to proceed. If the therapist won't speak to you or if you have questions that remain, a consultation with another professional may well be in order.

WHAT MOOD CHANGES CAN YOU EXPECT TO SEE?

"The first year of Katrina's therapy was hell," Grace and Jim Williams told us about their 16-year-old daughter who had had a long history of binge eating. They said:

> We expected that once she was in therapy, things would get better. But it didn't go that way. It was unclear what Katrina was doing with her eating. Sometimes she ate really healthfully—and then the next minute food would be missing and it was obvious to all of us that she was secretly bingeing again. But even worse, she became a complete misery to be around. Suddenly she decided it was okay to tell everyone what she thought of them; going way beyond being honest, she was really nasty. Her moods

were intolerable—one day sullen, one day angry. We just
wanted to stay out of her way. Things got a lot better after
the first year, but that beginning time was horrible.

Katrina's family's experience differed from that of Alice's, an 18-year-old in treatment for bulimia. Alice's moms told us that when Alice started to see someone, it was as though a black cloud had been lifted from the whole family: "Her mood brightened. She was visibly relieved, which made us all feel better."

There is no way of predicting how therapy will affect someone. It is a time when new behaviors will be attempted and new emotions come to the surface.

HOW TO BE HELPFUL

How to be most helpful to someone in treatment will vary from person to person. One 24-year-old woman, Jackie, told us that she felt badly that her parents never asked how she was doing in therapy. It made her feel ashamed about going to treatment, as if she was an embarrassment to everyone. Her parents, on the other hand, wanted to know how she was doing, but were afraid that if they asked Jackie would get angry. (It wouldn't be the first time they had been told to mind their own business.) So Jackie and her parents silently misunderstood one another and uncomfortably walked on eggshells whenever they got together.

If someone you know is entering therapy, ask them how involved they'd like you to be. Can you ask them how they are doing? Would you be able to join them for a session if you're worried about something? Discuss your feelings openly, and be willing to hear and talk about whatever answer the person in therapy gives you. Together you can anticipate how you'd like to handle potential difficult spots before they arise.

WHEN YOU'RE NOT SURE ABOUT THE PROGRESS OF THERAPY

As with the Williams, it is sometimes hard to believe that therapy is doing any good for the person you know. Perhaps they are still thinner—or heavier—than you think they should be, still bingeing or just, seemingly, no better than before.

Depending upon the severity of the situation at hand, your role will vary. No question, if you witness harmful behaviors that you don't think the team is aware of or if you feel no forward movement is being made with eating or weight, you need to let the person you care about know that you need to speak with the team. It is okay for you to let professionals know when you are worried. This is not a breach of the treatment. You need, in return, for someone on the team to speak with you and to feel like you've been heard. Often the team is aware of the problem and can explain what the treatment plan is regarding the problem at hand. Sometimes they won't know. Remember, you are the one in the trenches, most closely witnessing what is happening at home. If recovery is going to happen, everyone needs to be in communication about behaviors, concerns, and what happens next. It is possible, when you speak to the person you care about, they might tell you that they are happy with their therapist and that they feel like they are moving forward. However, if you remain concerned, you need to tell them that you are worried and that you need to let the therapist know your concerns. The therapist should have a clear plan of action regarding symptomatic behavior. They should be able to explain clearly why treatment should continue and what goals are currently being met. In more severe situations, the therapist should have a plan that involves the need for more intensive treatment if symptoms don't abate.

If your concerns are not addressed, insist on a meeting with the therapist and the person you are worried about. Or see another professional for a second opinion.

However, the therapist may explain that, as long as the person is medically stable and a treatment plan is developed, the work may be slow and the symptoms may not change as rapidly as one would like. In these situations, it might be best to pull back and not force the issue. The door should be left open to reassess the situation as treatment progresses. But at this point, it is not the time to insist on a change in therapy.

If you're paying for the therapy, you should anticipate this possibility beforehand and be prepared that even though *you* may not like the results, if the person in therapy and the treatment team is encouraged, at least in the initial phases of treatment, it is important not to interfere. Often the changes that occur are subtle at first and will be much more noticeable to the person in therapy than to anyone observing them. If you continue to remain concerned, however, a second opinion with a professional well experienced with eating disorders may be in order.

For some, therapy is *not* going to help with the eating disorder. In fact, treatment follow-up studies indicate, sadly, that approximately one-third of patients diagnosed with eating disorders remain unchanged symptomatically, despite clinical and psychopharmacological interventions.[3] The recidivism rate for binge eating is even higher. If someone has been in multiple therapies or has been in residential treatment over and over again with no sustainable change in the eating disorder, you may be facing this kind of poignant situation.

In these cases, despite a lack of progress with the symptoms, the goal is to use therapy to enhance the quality of the person's life, despite the ongoing presence of disordered eating and weight issues. Here, if the person indicates that the treatment is beneficial, it is important to encourage them to continue. As upsetting and exasperating as it is if someone does not change the disordered eating or thinking, it is possible nonetheless for someone to carve out a meaningful life for one's self. Therapy can help pave the way for other life goals to be reached in spite of the ongoing struggle with food and weight.

WHAT IF NO THERAPIST IS THE RIGHT ONE?

Sometimes, no therapy ever seems to progress. Someone may jump from therapist to therapist, program to program, disappointed that no one can help. Sometimes the person you care about has a very deep sense of dissatisfaction with everything and everyone around them. They are overwhelmed by their own pain, and if they go to a therapist, it is with the hope for a process that is swift and painless—a magical solution to the problem.

Therapy, however, is not magical. The process of developing a relationship with a therapist can be difficult and anxiety-ridden, especially for people who have little capacity to trust others. The process of knowing themselves better can be frightening and foreign, and they resist it at every turn. No matter what type of treatment is ultimately undertaken, there must be a commitment on the patient's part to the work. When the patient cannot make this commitment, the therapy will not succeed.

But even when the commitment is made, for reasons no one quite understands yet, some people just cannot be reached, no matter the care that's involved. They continue on a chronic course of disordered eating. Problems will likely exist in many areas of their lives and therapy will not be of much help.

For family and friends, these situations are most difficult. The helplessness and frustration that this type of situation engenders are enormous. No matter how severe the situation, there is nothing anyone can do to make a person stick with or benefit from therapy. Medical hospitalization can be utilized if the situation becomes an emergency, but you cannot force someone to change.

It is a terrible experience to watch someone you care about suffer and know there is nothing you can do. Your life inevitably has been relentlessly changed and a sense of loss as to what could have been pervades.

As hard as this is, if you are facing such a crisis, it is critical that you remember there are still other parts to the person you care about, moments you can connect, moments you can enjoy. When Michele Siegel (the co-author of this book) was diagnosed with what turned out to be terminal metastatic cancer, she was furious that suddenly everyone treated her like a cancer victim. "It's as if everything else about me has been forgotten," she said. "There's so much more to me than the fact that I am sick."

Remember Michele's words when you consider the person you care about. No matter how sick they are, they are not just eating disordered. This is hard to remember, particularly when someone is dying and still won't eat. Get support, talk about the complex feelings you have, find others who are going through what you are. Do not go this alone. It is time for you to seek help for yourself. But it is also time to continue any relationship you can with the person in trouble. If the eating disorder didn't exist, what else would there be to this person? Find those qualities, reach out and connect as best you can.

WHAT ABOUT YOU? TAKING CARE OF YOURSELF

Whether your situation is as critical as just described, or whether your concerns feel minor by contrast, you are still going to be left with questions, concerns, and fears of your own. Of primary importance is what to do about food. Make sure the treatment team is ongoing in communication with you about how to handle meals, food, and shopping at home. If the person is not in treatment and you're not sure if a serious problem exists, read Chapters 4 and 5, and consider consulting a professional with expertise in eating disorders to assess your concerns.

Regardless of whether someone is in treatment, having to accept the reality of the problem, the limitations of what you can do, and the limitations of what you can expect from therapy can leave you frightened, angry, and worried. You will need a place to voice your concerns and to learn how to make an independent life for yourself. You will need support regarding how to deal with eating issues as they arise. In fact, you may well be struggling with illness, death, or serious life problems of your own. Because you are trying to help the person you love, don't forget about yourself. The best thing you can do is to be a strong anchor for the person to come home to. We have found it invaluable for parents, partners, and even friends, to talk with professionals, other parents, or support groups so that there is a place for you to be attended to. Please don't go it alone.

PART III

USING NEW STRATEGIES

7.

WHAT TO DO ABOUT THE PROBLEMS WITH FOOD

Practical Advice for Those Difficult Moments

WHEN SOMEONE YOU CARE ABOUT HAS AN EATING DISORDER, REGARD-less of the treatment they engage in, you are bound to have questions regarding what to do about the food, weight, and body concerns. Each day you are living or interacting with the person you care about, and questions about what to do and say come up at every turn.

This chapter anticipates some of the difficult moments you will be inevitably going through and offers practical advice on how to best proceed.

Here, the goal overall is to engage with the person in ways that will first allow for medical stability, but then encourage a sense of the person's own autonomy and their ability to know and communicate who they are and what they need. With each problem that arises, how can you best set the stage for recovery? The goal is not merely to allow someone to regain a healthy relationship with food, but to use the eating disorder as an opportunity for the person you love—and the relationship you are in—to grow and change in whatever ways are needed at that particular time.

Rule #1: Parents Rule! Clarity, Consequences, and Care

Are you as parents acting as parents? Are you doing all you can to be the authorities in the family and, whether you are living with the other parent or not—are you acting as a united front?

Martha and Fred had been married and had two children, a year apart, before they divorced five years into their marriage. They had joint custody of both daughters who alternated weeks with their parents. Martha and Fred kept a distance from each other, tolerating but hardly engaging each other, despite raising two children together. When the girls hit their teens, both ran into trouble with food and weight. Bingeing, restricting, vomiting, and intense exercise seemed to keep each of them competitively linked in their attempts to be the skinniest.

Treatment was begun for both girls, with a key part being the dietician's urging for there to be three meals and two snacks daily.

Martha ran a tight ship, speaking weekly to the treatment team, shopping for healthy food, making sure the girls ate breakfast and dinner at home and left for school with a well-packed lunch. But at Fred's house, chaos reigned. Fred worked long hours on a construction team so he was rarely home. He thought the structure of the meal plans was ridiculous—as a teen, no one ever told him what to eat. And anyway, wasn't this just a crazy phase the girls were going through? They surely looked fine to him in their thin, toned bodies. So whatever Martha put into play during her time with the girls completely fell apart when the kids stayed with Fred.

Martha was furious and the treatment team frustrated while

the girls quietly rejoiced at their release from prison, as they called it.

If there is more than one carer in the picture, recovery almost definitely will be thwarted unless there is agreement as to how to proceed with treatment goals and food plans. In the example above, Fred and Martha actually had to meet with a therapist for weeks on their own to figure out how to be responsible and united parents. Fred had to be convinced that the girls were indeed in trouble, so that he could get on board supporting the work of the treatment. On the other side, Martha needed to quiet her anxiety and to talk with her daughters about what was needed instead of just demanding their compliance. Fred could actually support Martha in that regard, reminding her that sometimes talking with the girls or even letting things go would be a better idea than getting into the prison-like controlling homelife that she had begun to establish. In every couple, someone's seemingly worst traits can turn out to be just what the other person needs. Only when there was a more united front, and Martha and Fred were able to better support one another, was the family able to establish that the parents were indeed parents and that there was a plan of action that needed to be followed.

When parents stay steady as parents, with a clear message from both, doors open for the possibility of recovery.

Cathy, 14 and recovering from anorexia, was just out of a four-week residential facility, involved in an intensive outpatient program, but was already rapidly losing weight again. Five pounds less than when she came home, Cathy knew that if she lost one more pound, she would have to do a U-turn and return to the residential program for continued care. She was scared and determined not to go back to residential care but described mealtimes this way:

> I know what I have to do but I sit at the table and I just can't get myself to eat. In my head, I hear voices saying "You are a pig. You are going to get fat. You will be heavier than anyone else who's come out of the hospital program." My parents go crazy. They start to plead with me to eat. That only makes things so much worse. First, I'm in a fight in my head—and then I'm in a fight with them because I just want them to be quiet.
>
> If I'm going to even take a bite it has to be because I've dared myself to do it—to just take one step into the water. The second I hear their voices, I just shut down.

The first time out of residential treatment, Cathy let the voices win. When one more pound was lost, as her parents and the team had decided, she was readmitted into the residential program. The next time around, she hovered at her minimum goal weight. While her eating stayed fairly rigid, the fear of the consequences balanced the fear of eating. Cathy stayed out of residential care, maintained her weight, and was able to return to school and continue to build her life. Her parents' clear message that restriction had consequences kept the family from getting stuck in control battles and allowed Cathy to decide how to continue the work of her recovery.

We're often asked why we're not just focusing on the causes, the reasons why someone is struggling with food and weight? *If the real reasons don't only have to do with food and weight, why is the focus on setting limits? Isn't that just missing the point?* These are really important questions. Understanding what psychological purpose the disordered eating and thinking holds for each person is a critical part of any treatment. But when medical stabilization is needed, when health is at risk, words don't work. At these times, words and understanding only begin to have effect when the destructive behaviors or restriction are not immediate ways of coping. Understanding and exploration should always be part of the picture. When and how this kind of questioning can be effective is the ongoing balance of treatment.

Rule #2: Accept Your Limitations

Indeed, in some cases, words, exploration, and understanding are exactly what is needed before behavior change even has a chance. One parent, Robert, told us about his now 18-year-old daughter, Migelle:

> *Our daughter, Migelle, had always struggled with eating and weight, even when she was a child. Migelle was way above the norm for her weight by the time she was eight. She seemed to always be eating. If we went to a friend's house, the first thing she'd do would be to look to see what junk they had to eat. Our house was clear of anything with sugar and my husband, John, and I always ate so well. We really tried to set a good example—exercise, fruit. All the things we were told to do. Since Migelle was nine, we took her to so many doctors and tried so many diets. This may seem like we are so self-centered, wanting a thin kid. But Migelle had already been teased about her weight. She wouldn't put on a bathing suit or let us take*

pictures of her. Clearly, she was the one who was hurting. We really wanted to help her.

When she was 14, we pushed her to get on a weight-loss plan. We thought things were finally moving forward. Migelle lost 30 pounds. But then Thanksgiving and Christmas came, and by the beginning of the new year, Migelle weighed eight pounds more than when she had started to diet. Desperate, we took her to one more nutritionist who said to us, "Stop!"

She told us that we were not looking at Migelle and seeing who she was—we were trying to make her into someone she wasn't. "Stop trying to change her and get to know your daughter," she told us. Migelle was going to continue to work with the dietician and a therapist (her self-esteem was now on the floor). But the work was to better know Migelle, not her food. The goal was to help her listen to when she was hungry and when she was full. What was she feeling when she was craving food and wasn't hungry? What could she do instead to soothe, distract, or even know herself?

Our work was to try to know Migelle, to stop being the food police. Mindfulness when eating was to be a goal for the whole family and, of course, we were all encouraged to get off our screens and make sure we took walks and moved during the day. But we had to stop thinking we could change Migelle—because we couldn't. We started to realize that, previously, we had unwittingly been giving her the message that she wasn't beautiful, that she wasn't good enough, that she was a failure.

Migelle's weight didn't improve much for a couple years. But by the time she hit her later teens, we noticed she was indeed making better choices, going to gym classes without prompting, and she began to look healthier. More importantly, we had saved our relationship with her (which had been plummeting into daily control battles) and Migelle actually turned into a confident, feisty, and, most of the time, happy kid who knew her strengths and led with them. Had we kept up with the dieting programs, I fear her weight still would have been the same and we would have made sure that she was someone who hated herself.

And so, the second rule indeed is to accept your limits. This does not mean you do nothing. Migelle's parents very much had to start talking about feelings, not behaviors. They had to be supportive of Migelle and focus more on her strengths not on what they perceived to be her failures. It is a part of the recovery process that you let go of your own ideas of how someone should be and realistically assess who they are, what they are capable of doing, and what kind of help they need in order to take hold of their own life. In some situations, more active intervention will be needed on your part. In other situations, you will need to back off from monitoring the food. In either case, you are providing the groundwork so that their needs are heard, both by themselves and others around them. You are not merely making someone change. This is a subtle but critical difference. The person you *can* change is *you*.

Rule #3: Accept the Other Person's Right to Be Different from You

Maggie Johnson always believed that if anyone tried hard enough, they could beat the odds. Surely that's how she had run her life. Maggie was not unaccustomed to tough times. The daughter of an alcoholic mother, Maggie knew independence and survival from an early age. When her husband left when their daughter, Sarah, was a baby, Maggie worked hard to achieve the comforts she and Sarah enjoyed. Her strong commitment and sense of responsibility had been qualities that she had relied on throughout her life.

But when, as a teen, Sarah confessed to her mom that she was throwing up, Maggie's way of handling tough situations stopped working.

Maggie wanted to believe that they both could be strong women and fight anything. But nothing she did could make Sarah stop. How could Sarah be so weak? Sarah said she even wanted a therapist. How could a therapist help Sarah more than Maggie could? Maggie was heartbroken—and furious at herself for raising such a weak kid.

Sarah insisted though and found a low-cost therapist whom she really liked. Maggie gave in but had a really hard time when the therapist told Maggie to leave all food decisions up to Sarah. That turned out to be much easier said than done.

"I'm used to doing things, not *not* doing things," Maggie said some years later. "It was a long, hard struggle to realize Sarah needed me in a different way than telling her not to throw up. I had to have faith that I had instilled enough strength in Sarah to fight the battle on her own—and win! The only way to let her know I believed she could do it was to let *her* do it.

SHARING A HOUSEHOLD

It is one thing to be focusing on treatment and recovery. It is a whole other ballpark to have to deal with issues that arise in normal day-to-day living. Household responsibilities, money and finances, social outings, and advice inevitably become part of the picture in any family or relationship. When someone has an eating disorder, these issues can be all the more complicated.

In this chapter, we'll refer again and again to the rules that we've just spelled out as guiding posts when you face the question of "What do I do now?"

The goal throughout is to use the eating disorder as an opportunity to evaluate what the family or relationship needs now, so that you are doing all you can to set the stage for recovery while at the same time allowing for each person's individual needs for growth, connection, communication, and privacy to be better heard and attended to.

Household rules will differ depending on your relationship to the person who is in trouble with food. If the person struggling with food or weight is your son or daughter, you are in charge of the household, but their age will determine the kind of rules you establish. In a marriage, one partner does not make rules for another. There is give and take that ideally establishes a comfortable arrangement for both people. For roommates, expenses and household responsibilities are shared jointly by everyone living in the house.

Everyone who lives with someone who has an eating disorder must consider details regarding how and what food is kept in the house. There is enormous confusion about the solution.

Some people we've spoken with keep the house bare of binge foods like sweets, pasta, and bread, hoping the bingeing will be curtailed by the absence of such foods. In other households, closets are locked to keep food safe from the lure to binge. Still others keep the house well stocked, hoping having food around will keep someone from feeling deprived. And in some households the missing food is simply replaced and everyone pretends as though nothing is amiss.

Rule #4: Don't Purchase (or Avoid Purchasing) Food Solely to Accommodate Someone's Eating Disorder Unless It Is Part of a Therapeutic Plan

Household food is to be shared by everyone. If someone is struggling with bingeing, it is important that you don't buy food just to accommodate a binge. However, other people in the home are not to be deprived of foods they enjoy to keep someone from bingeing and/or purging.

When the Mortons discovered their 16-year-old daughter Patricia was bulimic, Mrs. Morton stopped buying any snack food and went from shopping once a week to shopping three times a week so there would never be a big supply of food in the house at one time. This made Mr. Morton and their two sons furious at Patricia because there was no snack food at home. Besides, they argued, it didn't stop Patricia from eating what she wanted. She bought snack foods anyway or ate a lot at her friends' homes. What it did do was make Patricia feel even worse because now everyone was angry at her (including her mom who was trying to do the right thing, but began to resent the constant shopping).

If your son, daughter, spouse, or roommate is anorexic, you may be tempted to have food on hand that they once liked in the hope of enticing them to eat. Unless the person asks for this particular food or if it is part of a structured treatment plan, do *not* provide food with the purpose of seducing someone to eat. It likely just won't work.

It is crucial that the person struggling with eating not be

the focus of the household's food decisions. You may feel like you are helping them by eliminating all sweets from the house. This is not help. What you are doing is preventing them from facing the seriousness of their problem and thwarting their motivation to do something about it. If the rest of the family doesn't want to have sweets around, that is one thing. But this decision should not be made just in an attempt to help the person struggling with food.

That being said, food that may be tempting to someone struggling with weight issues should not be on obvious display. One family always had glass bowls of Hershey kisses, peanuts, and candy decoratively placed all over the house. Yes, it looked good—but the only person who ate it was the teenage son who was struggling with bingeing. If others in the family want candy or sweets, so be it. But certainly don't keep them out on display; that's just too tempting for someone trying to make healthy decisions around food. Don't get rid of these treats if other family members want them—but do store them out of sight so they are not ongoing challenges to the person trying to make healthier choices.

In some households, particularly with roommates, it is helpful to establish food shelves for each household member. Each person chooses their own food and these become non-shared items. If these items are missing or eaten, they need to be replaced by the person who ate them.

The Mortons tried this and, in their family, it actually helped their daughter:

- Mrs. Morton would shop once a week. Common food would be kept in its regular place.

- Five shelves were marked, one for special treats for each family member, and the food on that shelf was only for that person.
- Mrs. Morton asked each week what everyone wanted for their shelf.

Everyone agreed not to eat food from anyone else's shelf unless they asked permission. If food from someone else's shelf was taken, it had to be replaced and paid for by the person who took the food.

This may well be extreme in most families. And of course, in the Morton family, the kids took food from one another's shelves and bickered about having to replace it. But for this particular family, the plan did something other than change eating habits. Here, the parents were trying to listen to each of their kids, and that listening in and of itself made the kids (despite the normal push and pull) all feel like they were being heard.

Rule #5: Unless Part of a Treatment Plan—Do Not Comment on What Is Eaten!

There are times when as a parent *all* you will be doing is commenting on what someone has eaten. This is a very structured part of parental re-feeding with a son or daughter who is anorexic or diagnosed as having ARFID. In a guided, caring, and unemotional (as much as that's possible) way, parents need to make sure all plated food under the structure of a healthy meal plan is eaten. Here, it is the parents' job to comment on what is eaten, to talk about weight, and to make sure the food plan is kept.

But when medical stability does not rule the treatment goals or when re-feeding is not part of the treatment protocol, what parents or loved ones should say is subtly different. Here the focus needs to be on the specific consequences that have been set regarding lack of treatment compliance. This would not mean pushing someone to eat more, but it may mean reminding the person that, without another pound gained, residential treatment may be needed. Remind the person of their strengths, of their courage, and ask how you can help them keep to their goals (even if the question is met with anger).

Your role is to support the person with their goals but *not* to push the food itself or to comment if they are not making a healthy choice. This is very hard and there is no question that there will be many times you blurt out what is on your mind, which will be some version of "Just eat it!" or, more fiercely, some version of "If you don't finish those potatoes, you're going to land in the hospital!" No parent will be able to be saintly about this. The most important part, is re-steering the ship, coming back to a more compassionate, supportive, but unemotional stance, letting your child know this is hard, but that you are going to support them any way you can to be strong and keep to their goals.

When someone is struggling with bingeing, again food shouldn't be withheld because it is fattening or unhealthy. You don't even need to say something for messages to be communicated. "When my family is having dinner, if I reach for a second helping, I can always see my mother watching me," Ruby told us. "She doesn't have to say a word for me to know that she is screaming at me to stop." Again, as a parent, it is so hard not to worry about your child's eating. No question your feelings will come across. Do what you can but remember—

making someone else's decisions about what to eat in the home leaves them unprepared for making those decisions outside the home. Questions like "Why don't you just take a taste of that?" or "Do you *really* want that?" are not helpful and should be avoided.

Jenny still struggled with bingeing when she was well into her 30s. She described what mealtimes had been like at home:

> *Mother would always prepare a diet dinner if I were pres-*
> *ent. I ate those meals—tuna stuffed in a tomato, no may-*
> *onnaise, or plain broiled fish and carrots—feeling like I*
> *was in a hospital. It made me so mad. I'd eat what I was*
> *served but all the while I was thinking about the cookies I*
> *had stashed in my room.*

Rule #6: Don't Force Family Meals but Make Sure to Have Time Together

In some situations, particularly when weight gain and medical stabilization are needed, family meals are critical. Here, there is a structure to when meals are eaten (at least certainly dinner), food plans can be kept and monitored when necessary, and most important, there is a reliable time for everyone in the family to connect. Studies show that family meals result in physically and psychologically healthier kids.[1]

That said, mealtimes can also be a time of extreme anxiety, distress, and control battles. Other studies show that screens (phones, computers, television) are now used at over 50 percent of meals.[2]

In a fast-paced culture like ours, family meals are often impossible. Kids have sports, parents work late, there are always meetings, events, or even friends that get in the way of dinner-time. What is the best thing to do about family dinners?

There is no question that having a reliable time to eat and connect in the evening is the best route to go. But (again unless there is a treatment plan regarding the food itself), forced marches can be worse than a predictable anchor of family time each night. Having healthy dinners available should be the responsibility of the parents. This may mean that meals are prepared earlier in the week for each night or that a plan of what will be ordered is thoughtfully mapped out each day. In many families it is not realistic that everyone will eat together and often it makes sense for kids to be able to order delivery or get their dinner from outside restaurants (particularly in urban environments). Some families make sure that at least one night a week is a family dinner. For others, if kids are making or ordering in their own dinners, there is a discussion regarding what the meals will be, what are good choices and how much can be spent. It is not a good idea for kids to be the ones responsible for their own dinners each night, particularly when the option is just ordering in.

Whether they are actually home or not, parents need to be involved with dinners—in planning, cooking, or monitoring what there will be. And if everyone can't actually be home for dinner, family time is needed regardless. As a parent, make sure you are connecting with each of your kids before the evening ends. As child and adolescent expert Dr. Ron Taffel notes, this likely won't be a calm discussion sitting down in the living room.[3] It more likely will be making sure you engage with your son or daughter when they stop you in the hallway and suddenly ask you an important question.

As for the dinners themselves—get off the screens! There

is a very high correlation between screen use during meals and junk food consumption during early childhood. What this means is that kids learn to focus on something outside of themselves as they are eating instead of paying attention to how they feel, what they are hungry for, and when they are full.

As parents, you also need to pay attention to your screen use. Work emails and event planning can wait. Television should be turned off. (Notice that this may be as hard for you as it is for the kids.) It is impossible to engage with the family when disruptions abound from all directions. As critical, it is impossible to be thoughtful and mindful about eating if you are not paying attention to yourself when you start to eat. How can you know that you are full if your attention is on the ball game in the background or the very funny TikTok video that is being passed around the table?

When you are eating, notice what's being said. Is the main topic of conversation food? If so, again, stop! What else can you talk about? In your head, go around the table. Notice how you feel about each person. Do you have a sense of who they are at that moment? What their day has been like? What are they feeling? In one family, it was clear that no one ever asked Dad what his day was like. In fact, no one really had any idea who he was outside of the family. One night, when pushed in a family session to talk about what his day was like, he actually teared up. No one ever asked him about himself. It turned out that day he had had to fire a man who was like a father to him. Had we not pushed, no one would have known.

Spend time each day being engaged and curious with your child or teen (or partner). In many cases, this will be just as important, if not more so, than a routinized fast-paced dinner during which no one really connects. We're in a much different culture than that of years ago when family dinners were a given. The goal now is to make sure thoughtful meals are available or planned, that there is an environment in which everyone is able to pay attention to how their body feels as they are eating, and to create a home environment in which connection is a given, be it at the dinner table itself or standing in the hallway. No matter where or when, it is the engagement and genuine curiosity about other family members that allows for the best possibility of connection and sets the best stage for recovery, not just for the person struggling, but for the entire family as well.

Of course, all of the above recommendations will be exceedingly hard if your child is seriously in trouble, starving, and needs to gain weight. Mealtimes will likely be hell. But using the above thinking as a guide, make sure even in the depth of interventions that you remember to pay attention to that person as a person, not just as someone with an eating disorder, and to remember to stay engaged with everyone else in the family. Everyone, including you, needs to pay attention both to eating thoughtfully and to connecting with others, the two guiding posts for surviving any meal.

Rule #7: Be Willing to Negotiate Household Chores Involving Food

Whenever someone with an eating disorder is living with others, the most mundane daily tasks can become difficult. Certainly, food shopping and cooking are two of the common household routines that can quickly be filled with anxiety for everyone.

Often questions arise about who should do the shopping

and cooking. In some households the person struggling with an eating disorder may have been the person responsible for cooking or food shopping (this is particularly true when a mom, or even a roommate, has an eating disorder). If this is uncomfortable for that person, consider what changes can be made.

In Ellie's family, Ellie and her dad lived on their own and she was responsible for the weekly shopping. When Ellie was struggling with bulimia, the foods she'd bring home would be all low fat, no salt, and sugar free. Her dad got furious. "What about me?" he demanded. But, of course, Ellie was wondering, "What about me?" After one particularly heated fight, they both relented. They decided that Ellie would do more work around the house and her dad would do the weekly shopping. "I was so relieved," Ellie told us. "It had been like sending an alcoholic to the bar to bring home booze. Every aisle had been a struggle to get through."

Rule #8: The Person with Disordered Eating or Purging Is Responsible for Their Behavior Whenever It Affects Others

BATHROOM MESSES

If someone is vomiting, they are responsible for leaving the bathroom clean and usable for the next person. This rule must be inflexible and nonnegotiable!

Mrs. Jackson agreed with this idea. Her daughter Sofia was just starting treatment for bulimia but had hardly stopped bingeing and throwing up. Just as bad, she had been leaving the bathroom she shared with her sister a mess after dinner, with vomit on the toilets. This always happened at night after

Mom went to bed. In the mornings, Mrs. Jackson would insist that Sofia clean the toilets. Sofia would say, "Yes, Mom," and "Okay, Mom," until she was going to be late for school but the bathroom remained dirty. That, of course, stopped Mrs. Jackson short—she didn't want Sofia to be late to school. Disgusted, Mrs. Jackson would end up cleaning the toilet herself—and be furious.

When we heard about what was happening, we were firm that things had to change. We assured mom that the bulimia itself might take some time to stop. But we were worried that Sofia was pulling her mom into a problem that Sofia alone needed to be responsible for. Recovery and taking care of herself were her goals, not her family's. Sofia had to leave the bathroom clean each morning and stop involving her mother in her eating disorder.

Despite Sofia's protests about this, everyone else agreed, both with the plan and with the fact that Mrs. Jackson was the authority. If Sofia didn't clean up after herself or if she were late for school, she would have no computer for that evening except for a designated time to do homework, within her mom's sight so that the constant barrage of messages and social media could be limited. We urged Mrs. Jackson not to get angry, but to stay firm. Computer time was no question a very valuable commodity for Sofia. Two days of uncleaned toilets—and, consequently, no computer—and Sofia finally started to change. Mrs. Jackson continued to feel worried about the fact that Sofia was vomiting, but she had made a significant first step in allowing Sofia to see that the purging was her responsibility and she had to decide how she was going to handle it.

You are not to take on responsibilities or ease the consequences of disordered eating behaviors. Such help prevents the other person from accepting responsibility and beginning to take charge of their own recovery.

REPLACING FOODS

If someone binges, they are responsible for leaving the kitchen clean and usable. This includes replacing the foods. If a binge has depleted household or shared supplies of food, these must be replaced in time to be available to others.

If someone feels they have free rein over everyone's food with no consequences, this can be an uncomfortably powerful position. One 17-year-old told her support group that she felt as though she was "getting away with murder" in response to her parents' continual replenishment of the food she ate. This was not a position about which she felt pleased.

A plan is necessary for how these situations are to be dealt with.

DEVELOPING A CONTINGENCY PLAN

Rules are useless if you can't enforce them. Along with making rules, you also need to have a plan in effect in case they're broken. What you can do about broken rules depends on your relationship to the person and their age. If you are the parent of a child who lives at home and is financially dependent on you, you have more authority and different options than if the person is your spouse or roommate.

The Simons, parents of 18-year-old Abigail, called us because their daughter continually woke in the middle of the night and binged and then purged on all the available food.

The Simons were so angry. On many mornings they opened the refrigerator to nearly empty shelves. The Simons felt they had no control over Abigail and were at a loss about what to do. They had been pleading with their daughter to get help, but Abi had refused.

While we didn't want to punish Abigail for behavior that clearly felt out of control to her, we did want to support her parents in finding ways for Abi to better deal with the eating. We wanted the Simons to have more authority in making sure their daughter got the help that she needed. And we wanted to make sure that they weren't walking around feeling helpless and enraged. The Simons decided that what could work in their family was to have Abi be responsible for the cost of the nighttime binges. Abi responded to financial rewards and penalties, so they decided to have a charge for the bingeing, an amount that would be deducted from her allowance.

Night bingeing is often terribly difficult to stop. The goal wasn't to punish Abigail into becoming binge free. The goal was to have her accept that this was a reality and that she had to take stock of what she was doing. In this case, Abigail got so frustrated that she finally agreed to work with a therapist—something her parents had been wanting but unable to enforce for several months. Once treatment was started, the allowance contract was dropped and the family worked together to find ways to better support Abi through the rough nights.

If the person you are concerned about is a friend or a spouse, negotiate a plan whereby the person you care about is responsible for their behavior.

Sophie and Caron were roommates. Caron's bingeing affected Sophie because Caron ate all the food. Sophie was furious but worried that saying something would embarrass Caron. We supported Sophie in talking to Caron. She had to let Caron know that she realized this was really hard to talk about but it was becoming a serious problem. Sophie asked that Caron buy more food for herself. Caron didn't want to do this because it meant that she had to acknowledge that she was planning to eat more than she wanted. When she ate Sophie's food, Caron said it was as if the urge just came over her unexpectedly. She had no intention to eat all that food, so she refused to plan for binges and buy extra. Sophie felt in a bind. Certainly, Sophie could not punish Caron. What she could and did do, however, was to let Caron know she was putting a strain on their friendship. If food was eaten, Caron had to replace it immediately— even if it meant going out or ordering food in during the middle of the night. If not, the friendship was at risk. The consequence of the bingeing was the breach that would ultimately occur if Caron would not be responsible in the agreement and the relationship.

In another situation between roommates, where the issue was a dirty bathroom, the roommates all talked to the friend in trouble. She was embarrassed but agreed to take better care. Ultimately, she actually agreed to pay for a cleaning person to come in a second time weekly. She knew that if she didn't keep to this contract, she would most likely lose her roommates and this was not something she wanted to see happen.

A contingency plan is like a business agreement. You establish in clear and simple terms what the agreement is. This includes spelling out what the actual consequences of behavior will be. The plans will change again and again. Remember, the goal is not merely to stop or change behaviors. The plan is a way of negotiating needs among everyone involved. This kind of negotiation is needed in any relationship. Here are some guideposts that can help:

- Use a contingency plan only in situations where the behavior directly affects you.

    Do *not* use it to control eating or purging behavior unless part of a well-thought-out treatment plan. Have consequences only for those behaviors that impact your day-to-day life.
- Be sure the consequences are realistic and enforceable.

    If you are parents of a minor, loss of screen time or allowance often helps. Remember, the goal is to support someone in taking better care of themselves, their family, their living community, and their relationships in general.
- Be consistent.

    If you give in and don't keep the agreement, the effectiveness of all future agreements will be lost. Be prepared to stick to your guns. And expect to be tested. At the outset of a new plan, the person will want to see if you really mean it.

    You may find yourself saying, "All right, we'll let it go this time but the *next* time our agreement holds" or "I would take away your computer but I know you need it for your homework." When you hear yourself saying these or, better still, thinking these phrases, *stop yourself.* Every time you avoid enforcing a consequence, you let the person know that it's not that serious and that your needs don't matter and, inevitably, you will stay enraged.

- Don't apologize for enforcing your plan.

  Expect an angry response and, when it comes, do your best to stay calm. You'll be told that what you are doing is making things worse. Hold tight, get support, and try to remind yourself that anger is almost always a part of the recovery process.
- Don't be shaming.

  This may be the most important rule of all. Someone who is starving, bingeing, or purging is in trouble. They really would stop it if they could. The *only* goal of talking and setting consequences is to take seriously that there is a problem, to get the help that is needed, and to limit how the problem is affecting others.
- Don't hold a grudge.

  Once you have carried through with your plan, try to put aside your anger. If the person is having a hard time keeping to the agreements, talk to them. Let them know it's hard. See if there's a way that you can support them in keeping to the plans.
- Plans are not made in stone.

  A plan must be flexible so there is a response to the individual's change. And remember too—none of this will go smoothly! Plans may change weekly. We're not asking you to be drill sergeants. We're asking you to keep up a dialogue in which everyone's needs are voiced and recognized. By establishing a plan, you are letting the other person know that you have needs too, even if they are the person in trouble at that time. The most important part is an attempt to talk about what is working—and what isn't. Your relationship and communication with each other are as important as any change in behaviors.

DON'T MAKE EXCUSES FOR THEM

Sometimes eating-disordered behaviors can have more dire effects than a messy bathroom or missing food. Loss of a job, loss of friends, or school problems may result from the isolation, self-consciousness, or preoccupation often connected with an eating disorder. Do not provide excuses or help cover up; you will only be prolonging the problem.

Laurie wanted to help when her roommate and good friend Carla asked her for a favor. Carla had a particularly bad episode of vomiting that left her with a very swollen face and in a very depressed mood. She did not want to face her colleagues at work feeling and looking the way she did. She asked Laurie to call her boss for her and to tell her boss that she was sick. Laurie did. Several weeks later, Carla asked Laurie to phone in again and tell Carla's boss that Carla had a bad stomach virus. Feeling unnerved by the whole situation, Laurie spoke to a friend who strongly advised Laurie to stop making it easier for Carla. The longer Carla could run from the fact that she was hurting and in trouble, the worse it was for her.

"It was a hard lesson," Laurie told us. "I thought lying for Carla was an act of friendship. Now I see that a real friend would not help her hide from how much trouble she was in. When she asks me, I tell her that because I care about her, I cannot help her that way. Right now, I'm trying to find a therapist for her to see."

Rule #9: Do Not Monitor Someone Else's Behavior for Them (Even If You Are Invited To) Unless It Is Part of a Well-Thought-Out Treatment

If the person you care about is in a medically compromised situation or if you are engaged in a family-based treatment plan in which your ongoing intervention is critical, then you must supportively monitor behaviors. This is often the first line of treatment for a child or teen who is starving. Even before professional help is sought, you may decide that your son or daughter's eating is a main priority and that the parental re-feeding is necessary. If you have opted to go in this direction, monitoring someone's food is obviously the main focus. The most important issue here is to assess what is working—and what is not. If the monitoring is not resulting in your child's moving forward with health and eating—or if it is tearing the family apart with fights—do not go this alone. Get a professional to assess whether you, as a family, need more support in taking hold of the food issues. Even if parental re-feeding is indeed helping with the food and eating behavior, pay attention to the feelings that get evoked by the intense work involved. In this type of approach, parents often put everything on hold to help their child recover. But know that, with this kind of focus, inevitably comes some degree of anger and resentment. If you are supporting your son or daughter in this way, make sure that there is a place to attend to your own feelings.

In some cases (as long as someone is medically stable), encouraging dependence can be crippling. This does not help the person to develop their own sense of control. In some cases, it may be more respectful and loving to support the person's own attempts at recovery than for you to act as an overseer. In these cases, professional guidance is of course needed.

No matter the severity of the problem, in general, it is not uncommon for the family or relationship to revolve around the eating disorder itself. A teenager may ask their parents to stay at home in the evenings so they won't be tempted to binge (an activity they will only do in private). In other cases, you may prefer not leaving someone vulnerable to the temptations of the kitchen. There is never a clear-cut answer as to what to do.

There are times when bingeing or purging is used by a child or adolescent as a cry for help that doesn't really have to do with the food at all. It may be a way of saying that they need more attention from their parents. Parents' decisions to spend time with their son or daughter should not be based on controlling binges but instead should be a way of responding to genuine needs for the time together. Sometimes just talking about the issue as a family can help; other times talking with a professional might be necessary to figure out what might be most important.

Rule #10: Watch Your Own Eating

Parents ask us all the time whether their attempts to eat well and stay fit have caused their child to develop an eating disorder. Parents who eat healthfully and exercise regularly, in fact, can be good role models for someone struggling with bingeing, starving, or compulsive exercise. In and of themselves, these activities do *not* cause an eating disorder.

Problems develop not from setting a healthy example, but from communicating how food is used by you and the person you care about. If you constantly use food to quiet emotions or to cope, there's no doubt your kids will learn to do the same. Pay attention—this is not about *what* you eat but *how* you eat.

Problems also develop when a family's way of eating doesn't allow for individual differences. Parents can set a good example, but children have to have choices as well. This is true for the child struggling with bingeing where a no-sugar rule can lead to more trouble, not less. A better alternative would be to have a rule in which kids are allowed to choose when they will eat sweets and what the sweets will be, even if a limit is placed on how much. This is also true in a different way for a child who is starving. For example, they may not have a choice about having to eat breakfast, but they may be able to decide whether they are going to have an egg or yogurt for their meal. (They will insist that they are not hungry for anything. Recovery will need to be in place for quite some time before they know what they really want to eat.)

Parents (usually moms of daughters) of a child on a meal plan to gain weight often wonder if they have to eat the same calorie-laden foods as their child. "I'm worried that if I eat less, it looks like I'm restricting, but I'm happy with my weight and what I eat," one mom told us. This is always tough, but the main message is that a big part of recovery is for everyone in the family to think of one's own needs in a self-caring way. That means that a daughter's meal may indeed look different from her mom's. It is a tough balance because there are times when the mom's eating an unwanted snack may really encourage the daughter's recovery. But if this compromises mom's self-care, then that will lead to anger and resentment, and won't help.

This is indeed a time to reckon with your own behaviors. Are you giving the message that there are good foods and bad foods? Are you eating more than you like? Are you restricting and not listening to your own hungers? Pay attention. While you may be trying hard to promote recovery, even unspoken thoughts about how to eat will be loudly communicated to the person struggling with food. While you don't have to eat the same thing as the person trying to recover, it is important that you know that your own rules about food and weight will be recognized. Be thoughtful about what messages you really are sending despite your best efforts to help.

Questions and Answers on Sharing a Household

The following are common questions regarding household rules:

Q. **I found my 15-year-old daughter's laxatives in the bathroom last week. She is in treatment for anorexia nervosa, but still uses laxatives to flatten her stomach when she eats. I threw them out. Was that the wrong thing to do?**

A. Don't go searching through your daughter's private things, such as her purse or drawers. However, if she leaves laxatives or other items, such as diet pills or diuretics, in a noticeable place like a bathroom shelf, then do remove them and comment. It may be a cry for help. Let her know that you found the laxatives. Tell her that you worry about her health and that you need to help her find a way to stop. Given she is in treatment, be sure that her physician and therapist are aware of the laxative use. Let your daughter know you need to speak with them and make sure they know your concerns. (If this daughter were not already in therapy, we would suggest reading Chapter 4, "No More Secrets," for advice as to how to proceed.)

Q. **My wife was hospitalized for anorexia nervosa. She's been out of the hospital for two months. The other day I noticed she had bought diet foods for the house and she's eating less at meals. The last time I called her therapist without telling my wife, she got furious at me. But I'm scared she's going to lose too much weight if I don't do something. What do you suggest?**

A. Tell your wife about the changes you've seen in her eating habits. Tell her how scared her behavior makes you feel. Say it is important that she do something about it, and suggest she speak with her therapist. Explain that it is difficult for you to stay out of her eating if she's not talking to her therapist about it. You need reassurance that she is aware she's having a problem. If you are in therapy together, bring this issue up in your couples' session. If the changes in her eating persist, tell her you will be contacting her therapist—but make sure she knows you are going to call. Likely the therapist will just listen and won't be able to respond directly, but you don't want to stand back and not pay attention to the likelihood that your wife is in trouble.

Q. **What about having a rule that our daughter can do whatever she wants outside of our house, but in our house no bingeing or purging is allowed?**

A. Only make rules you can enforce. Unenforceable rules make you ineffective, and the more of them you establish, the worse the situation will become. Our experience is that trying to stop your child from bingeing and purging will only result in sneaky behavior and won't change anything. Remember, this is not something that someone wants to be doing. They are turning to food because they don't have other ways of dealing with feelings. They get rid of the food because of extreme insecurity they have about "being fat." Stick with the rules that ensure someone is getting help and that focus on actual behaviors in the house. And make sure you talk with your son and daughter, letting them know that they can turn to you if they are having a rough time.

Q. **My husband and I are divorced and my daughter is in recovery from anorexia. She has a meal plan that she is supposed to follow. When she is with me, I make sure I see what she eats but my ex thinks that's too intrusive and we should just trust her. I trust my daughter—but I don't trust the anorexia. What should we do?**

A. Parental agreement, whether parents are living together or not, is one of the most important factors affecting the recovery of children or teenagers. Developing a united stance is the place to begin. If you both can't give your child a clear message, you may need some support from a therapist or group in this regard.

Ultimately, you may not be able to do anything to change your partner. In this case, you must establish rules that you will keep to in your house, regardless of what your ex-husband does. The message to your daughter should be clear though—with or without her dad's support, if she loses weight, she most likely will need more treatment or a higher level of care.

Q. Our daughter is 25 years old and binges and throws up often. She eats everything in the house and leaves the bathroom a mess. All our attempts to make her responsible for replacing the food or cleaning up her mess have failed. She refuses to go into therapy. What can we do?

A. As parents, you have a large degree of leverage in terms of ensuring that your daughter gets the help that she needs.

The most important thing is that your daughter is in trouble and the first message needs to be that you care and want her to get support. She is making it clear that she is having a hard time. Sometimes it's much easier for kids to anger their parents than it is for them to recognize they need help. Consequences for lack of responsibility around the house is a first step. Talk to your daughter about what is needed, both regarding responsibilities around the house but also regarding treatment as well.

Having your daughter, or the whole family, speak to a professional is likely needed. If she refuses to see someone, then you as parents need to meet with a therapist or support team who can help you better understand why your daughter is in trouble and what can be done about it.

By not responding to her negative behavior, you are giving her the message that you don't care about the part of her in trouble.

Q. **In our family, we have begun using separate shelves for each person's favorite foods. However, our 15-year-old daughter is constantly buying food that she doesn't eat. If she is going to buy special foods, shouldn't she be responsible for not letting these foods go to waste?**

A. Someone with an eating disorder is initially going to feel awkward and confused about making decisions concerning what they'd like to eat. Your daughter is going to have to experiment with learning her own tastes, the amount of food she needs, and the types of foods she will enjoy or feel comfortable with. She may need to know that more food is available than she actually wants. Expect that food may very well go to waste at times. (You may put an upper limit on what gets spent.)

Q. **What should I say when my wife, who is trying not to binge or eat desserts, asks if she can have a taste of my dessert?**

A. Why not? Remember, it is not your responsibility to decide what she should or shouldn't be eating. If you are uncomfortable with this, you might tell her that you feel awkward given that you know of her wish to eat healthfully. Ask her what she feels would be most helpful for you to say in those instances. Don't feel that you need to know better than she what the best thing to say would be.

Q. **My partner is bulimic and in treatment for her disorder. When she shops for groceries, she doesn't buy desserts because she fears bingeing on them. However, she knows I enjoy these foods, as do our three children. Isn't it her responsibility to care about our needs, particularly those of our children, as well as her own?**

A. Not necessarily. There are times when one of the roles of being a partner or mother may not be able to be carried on as usual. This is one of them. Sending someone who is eating disordered to buy desserts is not unlike sending an alcoholic to a liquor store. This is a time when you should take over and be the one to buy desserts that you and the children like. While you need not be deprived of these foods, it should not be up to someone who is challenged by food and weight to have to choose desserts for the household. Food shopping may not be the best task for her. Maybe switch tasks if you can; have someone else do the food shopping and let her manage some other household chores.

Q. **My girlfriend and I have set up a program that I think might work. She has to tell me every time she binges. She initiated this idea and feels that just the idea of someone else knowing will help her to stop bingeing. It seems to be working. Should I continue doing it?**

A. It has been our experience that this is not an arrangement that works on a long-term basis. Initially, having to confess may make someone binge less. But ultimately no one likes to be controlled. What can happen is that, ironically, bingeing and purging can secretly increase as a way of rebelling against feeling controlled. There are other ways to show your girlfriend that you care about her. We recommend you back out of hearing her confessions about food. Instead of reporting her "sins," let her know that she can turn to you and question with you why this might be a rough time in general. That way, the goal is not stopping the eating but finding out who she is and trying to better connect with her at those times.

MONEY AND FINANCES

Interestingly, money is one of the hardest things for people to talk about. Even in therapy, patients are often more open about sex than they are about what they earn and what they spend. If you are in a position of either sharing expenses with or controlling the expenses of someone who is struggling with an eating disorder, then no doubt the eating disorder has provoked questions about money that may be hard to talk about.

One husband complained to us about taking his wife out to dinner. He felt as though he might as well throw $50 down the toilet instead of paying for food that faced the same fate. The waste of money infuriated him, but he didn't know what to do to change the situation.

A frustrated father wanted to know if he should reduce his 15-year-old son's allowance. The money inevitably went to food, and the father felt as though he was standing by helplessly, watching his son sink deeper and deeper into a pit of overeating.

Parents have asked us whether it would be indulging their

daughters' problems by financially contributing to wardrobes of varying sizes. One mother told us in a family session that she normally enjoyed shopping with her 17-year-old daughter Linda. At those times they could take off for an afternoon, have lunch together, and talk (and laugh!) casually as they went from store to store. Usually at those times, mom enjoyed being able to treat her daughter to a dress or shirt. Her daughter obviously appreciated that time together, too.

But in recent months, Linda's weight had been fluctuating wildly, up and down two or three clothes sizes. At this point, mom thought it was a waste to spend money on clothes that might soon be too big or too small and she wasn't sure if she would be encouraging Linda's weight obsessions by buying new clothes. The time together quietly came to a halt. Even the thought of shopping aroused too much tension.

Money presents a particular problem in relationships when an eating disorder is present. It is an area in which you may feel you have control that can directly affect the behavior of the person with the eating disorder. It is a part of the relationship that can easily be abused. And in so many cases the attempts to help the other person can turn into a misuse of this power.

Rule #11: Do Not Use Money to Control Another Person's Eating Behavior

Decide what would be appropriate behavior regarding payments, allowances, and shared expenses if the other person weren't eating-disordered. For a child or teenager, give an allowance that is based on their age and related to responsibilities in the house, not determined by the fact that they have an eating disorder. You might talk to parents of classmates to find out how other parents are handling spending and money with their kids.

In the case of the father whose son spends money on food, the father must decide what he feels is an appropriate amount of money for someone his son's age. If the son decides to spend his allowance on food, that is the son's choice. However, the father needs to be consistent and unyielding toward his son's inevitable requests for more money. This can be tough when the son asks for more money to go to the movies with friends; his father wants his son to have fun, social times. But, still, the father must stand firm.

Linda's mom had to decide whether she'd still like to treat Linda to a clothing gift (no matter what the clothing size). Maybe shopping for clothes was just too heated now. If so, Mrs. Hanes and Linda needed to pick another activity to spend time together.

No matter what the situation, talk openly and sensitively. Be curious about what the other person is feeling. And make sure not to offer money for pounds lost or gained.

We know of many families in which kids have been offered money for weight loss. This never works and only allows for potential feelings of failure. Additionally, it treats a serious eating problem as if it were simply a lack of motivation. This resembles a bribe and usurps the person's own inner commitments to making changes.

There *are* times when money can and should be used as leverage to encourage a child's seeking treatment for her disorder. This was discussed in Chapter 5 and is different from trying to control someone's eating behaviors. When money is considered as leverage, professional guidance should direct your behaviors.

If your spouse has an eating disorder, you will need to negotiate finances as a team and together come up with a plan that is mutually agreeable. The husband's questions about paying for dinners that his wife threw up should be answered in terms of the couple's mutual understandings and compromises regarding how money is spent in the family, not based on his wife's eating disorder.

Roommates and friends can run into trouble around money as well. Andrea had lent her friend Lynn $500 over the previous year for different weight loss programs. Ordinarily, Andrea would not lend out so much money, but she felt her friend was in trouble and needed her help. Lynn's failure to keep the weight off enraged Andrea, and she told Lynn if she did not lose 20 pounds within the next month, she wanted all her money back.

Unfortunately, it is not uncommon to find people embroiled financially in their friends' food and weight problems. Andrea was advised to make future decisions about whether or not to lend Lynn money in the same way she would decide this for other friends, and that the plan for payback of any loaned funds should be decided in advance.

We helped Lynn and Andrea work out a repayment system for the $500, whereby Lynn made monthly payments over the next 18 months regardless of her success or failure in losing weight.

In general, the overall task is to separate decisions about money from decisions that are made as attempts to govern, monitor, or control someone else's eating behavior.

Questions and Answers Regarding Money and Finances

Q. **My daughter has been diagnosed with bulimia. She spends all her allowance on food. I won't give her any more money when she asks me for it. I tell her that's all the money she gets and she has to make choices about what she spends it on. Then she goes to my husband and asks him and he always gives it to her. What should I do?**

A. It is important that you and your husband act as a team. You won't be able to make any effective rules if you don't back each other up. Talk with him about the message he's sending her by giving her more money. Tell him that you know your daughter's health is very important to him but that he's unwittingly infantilizing your daughter, not encouraging her to think about her own health or spending.

Ultimately if your husband still doesn't change, you need to stay steady and continue to keep your rules about money clear and predictable. Your husband will have to decide for himself how he wants to deal with his daughter. Your own clarity, despite what your husband does, will still be helpful. Remember the goal here is not to stop the behavior, but to send a message that you expect your daughter to be thoughtful about how she is taking care of herself, both with regard to food and to spending.

Q. **Money is missing in our house and we know our 17-year-old daughter has been taking it. No one else** has been in our home at all. We think our daughter is using the money to buy food that she's too embarrassed to ask us to pay for. My husband and I don't want to make her feel more ashamed because we know she is really struggling with bingeing. When we even suggest that money is missing, our daughter gets mad and cries, saying she can't believe we would even think this. But the money keeps disappearing. What can we do?

A. You are most likely right that your daughter is ashamed—both of the eating and taking the money. To start, make sure you begin to keep money locked up when you aren't home. Your leaving money around gives the message that this isn't really serious.

Then talk to your daughter. Tell her that you don't want to get into a fight about whether she took the money or not. But the concern about money made you realize that you are really concerned about her. See if she will talk to you about how she is doing. Let her know you want to be there for her. If she's not getting support, it may be time for you to speak to a professional about what should be done next in terms of your daughter's struggle with eating and the possibility that she is lying to you.

Q. When our son turned 16, we gave him a credit card. Our agreement was that he ask us before he used the card. For months he had been responsible about using it, but recently he has been ordering Seamless, taking Ubers, and buying sneakers and not asking us first. Also, we see the bills but never the shoes, so we think he may be selling them at school to get money to buy food. We just recently found out from him that he has been vomiting to make weight for wrestling but we also see him bingeing on junk. Why would he do that if he wants to keep his weight down for wrestling? We don't know which problem to talk about first. What should we do?

A. Whether or not your son actually is selling the sneakers, given he is bingeing and vomiting, it's clear he is stressed about something. To start, talk to him about this. Is he too pressured about the wrestling? Or maybe he is bingeing because something else is on his mind. Talk to him. And even if he rolls his eyes and doesn't answer, you are letting him know that you are there to talk—and that you will want to continue to see how he is doing. Maybe he needs the support of talking to someone other than you. Open that up as a possibility.

That said, he still is abusing his credit card privileges. Make it clear that even if he is having a hard time, he cannot abuse the agreements you've had about money. The next time there is a charge on it that you did not approve prior to the card being used, you will have to take away the card until your son wins back your trust.

Being caring and supportive if someone is having a hard time does not mean that limits can't be set.

Q. Our daughter is 26 years old and lives in her own apartment. She earns a good salary, but she still always asks us for money. We couldn't figure out where the money was going. She wasn't using it for vacations or clothes, and her rent isn't that high. We know she struggles with bingeing and throwing up. Now we're worried that she's using the money to buy binge food. She's still asking us for money. What should we do?

A. Decide how much money you feel is appropriate to give your daughter each month to supplement her own income. You can let her know that you are concerned about her struggle with food. Though likely if you say this, she is just going to get mad. Make sure you stay steady with the amount of money you give her each month and remember—the amount you give her should not be based on what she is eating. You can't stop her from bingeing by controlling the money. It is up to her to decide how she is going to use that money.

Q. **Our 16-year-old daughter was picked up for shoplifting food. Should we be responsible for the lawyer's fees?**

A. Of course you want to support your daughter. All of you must be scared. Most likely, a 16 year old is not going to be able to pay for a lawyer so it makes sense that you support her financially if you can. But make sure you are not just letting the situation go completely. You may want her to pay for part of the expenses or set up another consequence. Suspension of her phone or reduction of computer time might be in order. Shoplifting can be a sign of more serious trouble. Use this as an opportunity to talk to your daughter about other concerns she may be having and to question how you may be of some help.

Q. **I'm so mad at my wife. She has had an eating disorder since she's been a teenager and she says she is getting help for it but nothing seems to be changing and so much money is being spent on her treatment. She totally runs our home and is a great mom, but I'm the one who makes the money. That was okay for a long time but recently, it seems like things are getting worse. If I say something, will that make it worse for her?**

A. Talk to your wife about your concerns. It's okay that she knows you are worried. Urge her to have you join her with her therapist. Maybe you can better understand what you can expect from treatment at this point. You'll have to decide together what is a reasonable amount to put aside for therapy but how she uses the treatment may not be something you'll be able to control.

Q. **My roommate eats all the food in our apartment. We made separate shelves and our arrangement was that she wouldn't eat any of my food, but she does it anyway. I don't know why she thinks this is okay—it's not! What can I do?**

A. This is a tough conversation to have but let your roommate know that you need to talk to her. Tell her that you know it's hard to talk about but you don't want her to take your food. Of course, she should pay you for food she's taken, but the bigger issue is that roommates have to respect one another's needs. Let her know that you know this isn't easy for her. But this is really hard for you too and it is infuriating that she isn't thinking about you. If she feels she can't stop herself at the rough moments with food, it means she really isn't in a place to be sharing a space with someone else. If she keeps taking your food, you are going to have to plan to stop living with each other.

Q. My wife and I both work so she has her own paycheck, but we need both of our income to pay for our home and other expenses. Recently, I know she has been using a lot of money on food. I see the Seamless bills and restaurant charges. Some of the orders look like they come in right before I come home from work, right before we have our own dinner together. It's not fair that her money is going to binges and my money is what is taking care of us.

A. This is yet another hard conversation to have but it's important that you talk. Start by making sure your wife knows you are not trying to control what she is doing with the food but that you are worried she is having a rough time. Is there anything you can do to support her or to help her speak to someone if indeed she is in trouble with food. The most important thing is that you let your wife know that you think something is wrong.

But you also have to talk about money. See if it makes sense to set up a joint account in which each of you contribute a proportionally fair part of your salaries. But also make sure that you each have your own separate accounts for your own spending. In this way, you are letting your wife know that you want to be there for her and you want her to get help. But that day to day, she has to decide what to do with the money that is her own.

EATING OUT, ENTERTAINING, AND FOOD

Going out for lunch, dinner, a drink, or coffee is so much a part of day-to-day life that it's almost impossible to imagine how hard this might be for someone struggling with food or body image.

When Kathy first told her friends she was bulimic, they were afraid to suggest going out for dinner together. "Suddenly I had fifty offers to go to the movies. You can't talk to someone in the movies." Kathy's friends were walking on eggshells. This is common. After all, you don't want to make matters worse.

Janis's experience was at the other end of the spectrum. "Every time a friend suggested having a meal together, I would get panic-stricken. I was too afraid I'd put my friend off by saying no and I was terrified of eating in public. I would spend the entire week focused on the dinner, what I would do, what would I eat, would I vomit?"

Rule #12: Do Not Anticipate Someone Else's Needs. Ask!

You cannot know and should not anticipate what will cause someone else's discomfort. For example, clothes shopping can be as anxiety provoking as eating for someone preoccupied with body size. The only way to be sure is to ask. Be willing to negotiate. How can you spend time together that is fun and engaging? Imagine for a moment how you use food or alcohol to socialize. We all do. What would it be like for you if eating or drinking were taken out of the mix? Thinking about that may help you understand what it might be like for the person you care about.

Also, try not to take things personally. It is not to hurt you that the person is not eating. If you feel hurt, it means the food problem is escalating to a problem in your relationship (see Chapter 8). Respect that the person is unable to comfortably be in a restaurant situation; this is similar to a recovering alcoholic who does not want to spend time in a bar. When the person feels more in control, they may wish to resume this activity.

Rule #13: Don't Make Eating Out a Battle of Wills

This is tricky business if you love to eat out and a family member or friend doesn't feel comfortable doing that. Are there certain restaurants that feel more comfortable to them than others? Maybe they can read the menu in advance so that they will know what they can eat. Don't worry that this is not normal behavior. If someone is struggling with an eating disorder, it is not realistic to expect that things will be normal. If planning a meal in advance helps the person to feel easier about eating out, that is okay.

Often professional events are combined with eating and drinking. What should you do if you have to entertain for professional reasons and you want your partner to attend? What if they don't want to eat? Focus on their support in joining you—not on what is or isn't eaten. And don't push someone to eat in a certain way because you are worried what others are thinking.

But if for either of you it's just too uncomfortable, the best bet may be for you to go alone.

If you are a parent and your child refuses to eat out, you may decide not to take them with you when you go out to a restaurant. If your child is in treatment for an eating disorder, discuss with the therapist or team how best to handle these kinds of situations. Often a food plan may be part of treatment. You likely will need to make sure your son or daughter will be able to keep to their plan, whether they are at home or not.

Questions and Answers Regarding Eating Out and Entertaining

Q. When we entertain now, my wife won't eat in front of anyone. But after everyone leaves, she eats all the leftovers. She says she's too nervous to eat publicly. I wish she'd just relax and enjoy herself. What should I do?

A. The first question would be why does it matter? Be curious and talk to your wife about what you're concerned about. If in general she's not worried about her eating or weight, why does it matter? The most important issue would be whether she is engaging and involved with the people you are entertaining.

But talk to each other. Is entertaining stressful for her? Or is there a problem regarding food or weight?

One of the hardest things for anyone to do in any relationship is to just be curious. Talk to each other. Let your wife know who you are, what concerns you, what entertaining means to you. And listen to what she has to say. Questions, not answers or advice, may be the best place to start.

Q. **My wife is anorexic and in treatment. She's no longer at a dangerous weight but her eating habits are still pretty strange. She has a ridiculously long list of requests regarding how food needs to be made for her. And then when the food comes, she still cuts it into really small bits and pushes it around her plate. She hates going out to restaurants, but agrees to accompany me when I have to go for business events. To be honest, I'm worried about what my associates will think. What should I do?**

A. Certainly talk to your wife about this but it's likely if she could change her eating habits, she would. Hopefully that will change as treatment progresses and your wife feels more confident about herself.

For now though, you have a decision to make. If your wife isn't ready to change how or what she eats, you must decide either to have her accompany you and eat (or not eat) as she wishes. Otherwise, you will have to attend these dinners alone.

Q. **My daughter is in therapy for bulimia, but she still won't eat anything at family functions. Both my parents and my in-laws are asking me what's wrong. I've started making all kinds of excuses for why we can't attend, but I don't think I can keep this up much longer. What should I do?**

A. So many people are in this situation. Family members almost always ask what's wrong and you will want to be able to tell them. It would be best if your daughter could speak to the rest of the family herself, but that likely won't happen. You may feel that you need to talk about what is happening because this is affecting you, too. If you are close with someone who can be of support to you, let your daughter know whom you will be talking with. You need support, too! There's no question that, even if you tell one person (for example, your mom, your sister), your daughter is going to be furious. Make sure your daughter—and the person you talk to—both know that this absolutely should not be a conversation among family members.

If your daughter doesn't come to an event, it's okay to say that there are things she's dealing with and leave it at that. Encourage your daughter to speak to relatives on her own but don't expect her to go to every event. Let her know which family get-togethers mean the most to you and negotiate which ones she will attend. There may be times that you will have to go without her. But when she does join you, talk with your daughter about what (if anything) to say when you are inevitably asked why she doesn't eat. It's actually okay at those moments for your daughter to just say she's not hungry.

Q. **My wife is struggling with anorexia. Whenever we go to my mother's house or to a family function, my mother is always on my back about how little my wife eats. I've been begging my wife to please eat for my sake so I won't be put in this embarrassing situation. But she still won't eat and it's making things worse between us. What should I do?**

A. Your mother should not be involved in your relationship with your wife. Let your mom know that you are paying attention, that you appreciate her concern but that her asking about it isn't helping. Pushing your wife to eat will only create a control battle. It won't help at all with your wife's potential recovery. The issue here is really between you and your mother: how you can stay close to her but have privacy in your relationship with your wife.

GIVING ADVICE AND OPINIONS

People close to someone with an eating disorder tell us about the quandary they feel when asked for advice and opinions. Questions feel like potential pitfalls: "How do I look?" "What should I do?" "Am I too fat?" "Am I too thin?" How do you respond to such questions?

Rule #14: Do Not Get into a Pattern of Offering Advice or Opinions

Anyone who feels insecure about their body or what they are eating will often search for approval from those around them. It is very tempting to reassure them that they look fine or offer your advice about their eating habits, weight, or clothes.

These requests are signs of anxiety and insecurity. Your reassurances or suggestions may at best provide temporary relief. But in the long run, they interfere with the person's ability to develop their own judgment and self-worth. Of course, there are many times you might want to tell someone that they look pretty or handsome. And there will definitely be times when you'll answer someone directly. But if you find that there is a pattern of someone turning to you to figure out if they look good, it's time for that pattern to change. How can you support someone to be secure in their own opinions, thoughts, and judgments when they always turn to an outside measure of how they should be?

Josefine's mom was a designer and had amazing taste. She always knew how best to wear clothes and jewelry and her face always looked flawless. Her mom always suggested what Josefine should wear, no matter what the occasion. If Josefine put something together that she liked wearing, Mom would always comment, suggesting a small change—or a complete turn-around in what was appropriate to wear at a particular occasion. And indeed, Josefine was always the best dressed kid in the room. This was something she felt proud of. But as Josefine got older, she couldn't ever figure out what to wear, whether it was to school or to a fancy event. When she lived alone after college, she would send her mom pictures every time she got dressed to see if she looked okay. Unwittingly, mom's ongoing help had given Josefine the message that her thoughts on how to dress or look would never be right. Without outside advice to determine if she was good enough, Josefine literally could not get out of the house.

Rule #15: Do Not Comment About Someone's Weight and Looks

Telling someone with an eating disorder that she looks good or thin is not necessarily received as a compliment. To someone recovering from anorexia, hearing that they look good can sound like they're being called fat. And of course, if someone is trying to lose weight, saying someone looks good can communicate that previously you thought they looked terrible. This is tricky terrain because how someone looks now can generate a great deal of anxiety about how they used to look or how they will look in the future. While you may give a compliment in an offhand manner or mean it to be supportive, it can have effects far beyond your intent.

Barbara has struggled with bingeing for as long as she can remember. Her girlfriend of the past six months, Shelly, has been supportive of her difficulties, but recently, they ran into trouble. Barbara described the situation:

> I know this sounds overly sensitive on my part, but Shelly is always telling me when she thinks I look good. The other day she told me she thought I looked pretty thin—and it got me angry! It made me think that she must have thought I looked fat before that and then I was annoyed that she's always noticing. I'm worried enough about my weight as it is—I want her to be attracted to me but I wish she wouldn't make these comments. It makes me feel that if I'm not at a weight she likes, she's quietly criticizing me in her head. I feel like I'm under a microscope.

On the other hand, a dad told us that his now 28-year-old daughter was really angry that when she was growing up, he never told her that she looked beautiful or even pretty. "It made me feel like men must not like the way I look," she told him. The dad had actually purposely not said anything about looks because his daughter was indeed very pretty and he thought saying something would just make her focus on her looks.

A heartfelt joy about appreciating someone's looks is *not* advice and should be a part of any relationship exchange. Do not hold back if you are loving the way someone is looking—just don't focus on weight!

Questions and Answers Regarding Advice and Opinions

Q. **My daughter often asks me, "Am I too fat?" or "Do you think I should lose weight?" She is overweight and I've been telling her to lose weight, but nothing changes and I'm completely frustrated.**

A. Do not feel compelled to answer your daughter's questions. While you may care a great deal about her looks and weight, telling her so is not in her best interests. She definitely already knows how you feel and getting you to say so only increases her anxiety and concern regarding a subject about which, no question, she is overly worried. It is important that she determine for herself what her weight should be.

   Do tell her that you care about how she feels and that what is most important to you is how *she* feels about her weight. She has to figure out how she wants to look and what is standing in the way of her own goals.

Q. **My daughter has been struggling with bingeing and throwing up. Both my husband and I are very conscious about our appearance. It does bother us when she gains weight. But we don't want her**

to control her weight by vomiting. What should we do?

A. Don't make comments to her about how much she weighs. You may be putting a lot of pressure on her. Pay attention to how much you talk about weight and appearance in the family. How important is looking good to you? Sometimes your own family values may make it difficult for you to shift away from a focus on looks and weight. If this is your situation, you may need to work on deemphasizing the importance of appearance. Notice how many comments you make about your own weight or others. Do you say things like, "OMG, did you see Carole? She gained so much weight!" Those are the kind of comments that kids hear and take more seriously than you know.

   As important, it's obvious that if she is throwing up, she is in trouble. Talk to her (as we spelled out in Chapter 4). It is likely she is having a hard time and may need the support of a professional.

Q. **My husband eats constantly. He was a very heavy child but lost weight before we got engaged. Now he is gaining weight steadily. He asks if I'm still attracted to him. I say yes because I don't think it should be up to me to tell him to lose weight. But I'm not being truthful with him. Should I say anything?**

A. Yes. Tell him how you feel about his attractiveness to you. If asked, you might say, "I love you, but I'm more attracted to you when you're taking care of yourself. Right now, you seem like you are having a rough time,

I feel sort of shut out and that makes me pull away."
(We know people don't really talk that way—put this
into your own words.) The focus here is on what is
happening in the relationship, not on the weight itself. If there has been a significant weight gain, it likely
means something is wrong—and likely whatever that
is affects the relationship. Use your concern to question what else might be needed between the two of
you. Do not focus on the weight alone.

Q. **My daughter has been a really large kid since she
was born. Weight Watchers just came out with a
new program for kids. She wants to go and she
wants me to come with her. I want to lose weight,
too, and she says it will be easier to do it together.
Do you think that's a good idea?**

A. Weight Watchers indeed has recently developed a program specifically for kids and teens. By the time you
are reading this, it is possible the program has changed
or evolved. But unfortunately, studies show that putting kids on weight-loss programs do not work. Over
90 percent of kids gain back any weight that's been
lost—and sometimes more. Weight-loss programs almost always lead to yo-yo dieting and endless feelings
of inadequacy and failure.

　　If your daughter has been large since she was born,
as hard as this is to hear, it is likely she is going to
remain a large person over time. A better route than a
diet would be support that your daughter could get in
listening to when she is hungry, finding ways of dealing with emotions other than turning to food (if she

does so), and focusing on the parts of herself that she loves, not the parts that she wants to get rid of (i.e., her body).

As far as your dieting with her? Don't! Imagine how she will feel if you lose weight and she doesn't? Or, she could feel guilty if she loses weight and you don't. It is important that you each decide individually how you want to take care of your health. What is good for you may not be good for your daughter. Anyway, a big part of your work as a parent is to help your daughter separate from you and find out who she is as an individual. Thinking about how she wants to take care of her body is a good place to start.

Q. My teenage daughter thinks she's too fat to date, and so she refuses any boy who asks her out. I keep trying to tell her she looks fine, but she won't pay any attention to me. What should I do?

A. The extent of your daughter's insecurities is likely beyond the help of a little reassurance. There is nothing you can do to make her date. Talk to her about her fears, what concerns her. Focus on the strengths and beauty that you see in her. But if she's not getting professional support, let her know that things shouldn't be this hard. Tell her you want her to get some support with this and get the names of some therapists she could talk to. Let her know you want her to at least meet with someone. She sounds like she is hurting and you don't want to look back and feel you didn't do anything. And remember, as we've been saying, a weight-loss program is not going to reach the reasons why your daughter is having a hard time.

Q. **My roommate, who has bulimia, keeps breaking dates whenever she feels she is too fat to go out. She just wants to stay in and spend time talking with me. She's been asking me whether I feel she is inconsiderate when she does this. What should I say?**

A. Tell her that of course she is being inconsiderate, but you get how she is feeling. Is she getting help for the eating disorder? Your work as a friend at this point may not be just to spend time with her but to make sure she is getting the help she needs. Tell her you'll help her find a support group or a counselor at school to talk to. The best date night she might have with you could involve a professional therapist.

8.

WHEN IT'S HARD TO CHANGE

Why We Keep Doing What We Do—Even When It Doesn't Help

I T IS THE RARE PARENT WHO DOESN'T TRY HARD TO DO THEIR BEST when parenting their kids. And anyone in any relationship, be it a partnership or a friendship, wants the relationship to work. We do what we have learned from our own families—or we try to undo what we have learned—in order to allow for connection, intimacy, growth, and joy. But often the rules we have learned interfere with the very goals we have.

The Browns had a clear picture of what was needed to be successful in the world and in relationships. But they had a hard time knowing when or how to help their teenage daughter Tracey, who was in treatment for bulimia. The therapist had met Tracey's parents and had encouraged them to give Tracey time to deal with what Tracey called "her behaviors." But Tracey's parents weren't sure this was the right thing to do. "If she would just make up her mind to stop, she could," said her dad. "She's being stubborn."

The idea that the bulimia was more powerful than Tracey's willpower was contrary to her parents' values. Her dad had made it professionally as a successful attorney after an impoverished childhood. He had put himself through law school at night while working days. Her mom had raised her three daughters and then went back to teaching, the profession she had left to marry and raise her family. The Browns had overcome many obstacles in their lives and they saw Tracey's problem as resulting from a lack of self-control. They were determined to help her in the ways they believed would work.

No matter how many times they were prevailed upon to leave the problem to Tracey, they could not let it go. There always seemed to be another strategy they hadn't tried. They tried to reward Tracey with a shopping spree if she were to stop throwing up. They promised a trip. They took away her phone when they saw vomit on the toilet. The Browns felt that if they persisted, they could get Tracey to stop. But nothing worked. Both parents felt powerless—and quietly enraged.

Tracey dropped out of treatment and tried hard to cooperate with her parents' attempts to help her. Her parents were trying as hard as they could to help. They were doing their best but for years remained entangled in Tracey's problems.

Tracey lives on her own now, but talks to her parents daily about her eating habits. She lets them know when she's had "good days" and when she's had "bad days." Tracey's eating problem has remained the focus in her relationship with her parents—a focus that prevents both sides from separating and growing.

There are many reasons why it's hard to change. For the Browns, changing their attempts to help meant failure, giving up, that they were bad parents. Alternately parents and spouses find that, without realizing or intending it, they have somehow become oddly dependent on their son or daughter's illness. One mom we spoke with, noticed that when Wendy, her 16-year-old daughter, recovered from anorexia, it was hard for her and her husband to go back to what their life had been before Wendy's illness. Their marriage had revolved around Wendy. Now that Wendy was independently going about her life, her parents had to work hard to rebuild a life together. Brenda, Wendy's mom, spoke about it this way:

> We hadn't talked about anything but Wendy or done anything but worry about her for so long. In therapy, we were actually given assignments to spend time together talking about anything but our daughter. Because we'd been so involved with Wendy, it took an "outsider" to remind us that our own marriage was being neglected. The therapist was able to suggest specific things we could do that would help us be a couple again, not just parents.

Each family and relationship is different. Often the family's strengths are also their weaknesses, and change is hard for anyone, in any relationship. If you find that no matter how hard you try to change, you keep returning to old problems, this is not a sign of weakness or failure on your part. But, as in any situation, a challenge is also an opportunity. In this case, if you keep returning to old patterns of behavior, it is an opportunity to question what meaning the involvement has come to serve in your life. Perhaps worrying about someone else keeps you from facing even more difficult problems. Perhaps you are relating to a son or daughter the way you have been taught to behave with your own parents. Or maybe you are trying to do everything your parents didn't do. Maybe you are determined to help your child lose weight because you suffered so deeply as a teen for being large. You don't want them to go through the pain that you did. Involvement almost always means that you care. How to best be involved is always the question at hand.

One mom we spoke with had a 15-year-old daughter, Nicky, who was in treatment and working at resolving a three-year struggle with bulimia. Nicky's mom, Ginny, attended a parents' support group with her husband. They both wanted to do what was best for Nicky, but Ginny was having a really hard time.

> I've stopped asking Nicky what she's eating and if she's getting sick," mom told us, "but I still go into the bathroom after she's left it to see if there's any throw up. I find myself lying in bed at night waiting to hear if Nicky is in the kitchen. Lately I've even begun to look through the waste can in her room for candy wrappers or other signs of a binge.
>
> I want to stop, but I can't. I must be somewhat to blame for her eating disorder. She is my kid. I keep wondering if I focused too much on her being thin or if I kept too much food in the house. When Nicky was young, my husband, Michael, and I fought a lot—maybe that did it—making her feel insecure. In any case, I can't get it out of my head that I brought this on somehow. How can I just sit back and not do anything to make her better?

Ginny felt she was to blame for Nicky's behavior. She really believed that to stop tracking Nicky's every move meant that she was yet again not being a good mom. And of course, Nicky felt mom's endless worry and concern, but it made Nicky mad. Even though Ginny had definitely cut down on how much she said to her daughter, Nicky (like all kids) picked up on her mom's endless anxiety. Nicky felt intruded upon and found herself sometimes bingeing and throwing up to get back at her mom. It was hard at times for Nicky to remember that the bulimia was her problem not her mom's. It took a lot of time and work for Nicky and mom to each think about their own needs and feelings, not just to react to what the other was doing or wanting.

For another mom, Jodie, involvement felt like a life-or-death issue. Her daughter, Maddie, 18, had just been sent home from freshman year at college. She was five foot seven and 103 pounds. When Jodie saw her daughter, she was terrified. But, luckily, Maddie was also scared and began to eat a bit more as soon as she arrived home. A physician and treatment team decided that they would begin treatment on an outpatient basis. This was a complicated decision because Maddie was in a medically precarious place, but Maddie was motivated to gain weight at this point and had never had any treatment before. As a first step, appointments with a therapist, dietitian, support group, and physician were set in place weekly. The dietitian, who would be weighing Maddie, set out a meal plan that would allow her to gain at least a pound a week. Jodie met with Maddie and her therapist frequently, too.

Jodie's role was to provide food for Maddie's meal plan and to support Maddie in her efforts to eat. And, of course, to be clear that if Maddie didn't gain weight, a bed was already in place for her in a residential program where she could get more support and structure. Mom was to be supportive and to sympathize with how hard this was for Maddie, but she was not to actively comment on what Maddie was eating, nor was she supposed to feed her daughter. Jodie reported:

It was so hard. Maddie would labor over every bite. She was keeping to the program and she really was gaining weight each week. But at every meal, I watched her like a hawk, ready to pounce if she didn't eat right. I kept making comments to try to get her to eat more or faster. There were so many fights. It just all seemed so slow. She'd take one step forward, then one step back. It was infuriating and almost impossible not to say anything. How do you just sit back and watch your kid die?

There is not a parent in the world who doesn't find this kind of critical situation frightening and enraging. Jodie had the most serious justification to want her daughter to push forward more quickly. Without sticking to the meal plan, Maddie could die. But there were several reasons why Jodie was urged to pull back from the direct struggles over food. Maddie was an older adolescent who was indeed taking risks and eating more each week. And she and mom had an intense history of control battles in which Maddie would walk out of the room in the middle of a disagreement. Everything in this family's history indicated that mom's attempts to control the eating would be a disaster.

With a tremendous amount of determination and support, Jodie was able to let her daughter struggle to find her own voice regarding her own health and self-care. Maddie did indeed gain the needed weight to return to college—slowly and not without many challenging moments. But what Maddie and Jodie were able to learn from the crisis with anorexia was that Jodie had often done anything she could to keep her daughter from feeling pain. There was always a justification to come in and take care of her daughter. With a situation at hand that Maddie couldn't easily fix, both mother and daughter had the opportunity to witness Maddie start to take hold of her own life. With much fear and trepidation—and the support of a strong team working with them—Jodie allowed Maddie to take care of her own eating, move on, and return back to school.

WHEN HELPING HURTS

Sometimes it will be clear to you that your worries or attempts to help are not getting you—or the person you care about—anywhere. For others, the indications are more subtle.

Likely you've heard the saying that you are only as happy as your least happy kid. We do *not* expect that you will be able to stop worrying about the person you love. Nor do we expect that you will be able to follow a clear path in terms of what to do to help, but we want you to notice patterns. Notice how often you focus on the other person's difficulties. If you weren't thinking about their issues or the way they are behaving, what else would you be thinking about? What else *should* you be thinking about? What about you?

WHY WE DO WHAT WE DO

You may feel that your situation is different from others' and that there are good reasons for you to be involved, even if it seems to be making the situation worse. Nicky's mom felt that she was to blame for her daughter's problems. Shouldn't she be the one to make it better? Another woman, Paula, whose husband, Franco, binged every night, told us that she could not stop suggesting what he should eat because she knew he certainly wasn't thinking about it on his own. Paula was convinced that if she didn't say anything, he'd get so obese that he would jeopardize his health. "If he dies, it would be my business, wouldn't it?" she asked. "I mean, his dying would certainly affect *my* life!" This rationale kept her nagging her husband about everything he ate. The fear was understandable. The problem, however, was that Paula's involvement wasn't making anything any better. When Paula wasn't around, Franco ate whatever he wanted to.

Others stay involved because they feel convinced that the person with the eating disorder is doing this to hurt them. "If she cared about me, she would stop," is a phrase we frequently hear.

For example, John told us that his husband Alex knew how much it meant to him that he stop bingeing. If Alex loved John, he would stop overeating. John could not stop arguing with Alex about the food because he wanted Alex to see how he was ruining the relationship.

While every one of these people had their reasons for staying involved, the way they were involved wasn't helping. The attempts at helping only masked the more meaningful dilemmas and conflicts in their lives. Nicky's mom was having trouble sorting out her responsibilities as a mother. Was she wedded to some old ideas from her original family? Paula had work to do on why she felt her husband was so incompetent. Was he really, or was this how she was taught to relate to men and Franco was rebelling in response? John was measuring Alex's love for him by what he did or didn't eat. What kept him measuring Alex's love this way?

Involvement in someone's eating disorder is always needed.

The critical question is not whether you should be involved, but how. Sometimes direct involvement is critical for medical and emotional stabilization. But in other cases, the involvement should not directly focus on the food, weight, or eating. Other ways of being involved need to be considered.

YOUR INVOLVEMENT: WHAT IT MEANS

We know that there are different ways of caring and showing affection. Think of Gary Chapman's oft-quoted book *The Five Love Languages: How to Express Heartfelt Commitment to Your Mate.*

- Chapman believes that there are five different ways of expressing love: words of affirmation, quality time, giving gifts, acts of service, and physical touch. When one person gives love in a way that is different than what the other person perceives as loving, there's bound to be trouble. For example, if a father shows love by giving gifts but a child needs words of affirmation, both parties can feel misunderstood and wronged. The dad doesn't understand why his love is not being appreciated and the child can feel unseen and unloved.
- We see this kind of misunderstanding in all families, but when someone is struggling with an eating disorder, caring can be wildly misunderstood. Sometimes we try to care in the ways we were taught. Sometimes we feel that the way we were cared about in our own families was hurtful or misguided. Then we'll try to care for someone else in ways that we think are better. But not everyone experiences caring as it's meant to be felt.

When someone is in trouble and you are trying to help, it's an opportunity to learn more about yourself. What is your caring style? What works and why?

THE EFFECT OF FAMILY RULES

As we discussed in Chapter 3, old family rules may often guide the way we care and relate in relationships now, be it with a partner, with kids, or even with friends.

With Nicky's mom, her family rules made it hard for her to let her daughter struggle with her recovery without Nicky's direct involvement. For this mom, managing Nicky's food, managing whatever her daughter needed next, was mom's way of caring. Her own family rules were guiding or, more accurately, misguiding her behavior and care in relation to her daughter. In her family, not jumping in to fix the problem meant you were abandoning your daughter, not fulfilling your job as a parent—and certainly not showing love.

Friends and roommates can be in a particularly difficult situation in this regard. Imagine if you are living with someone whom you know is in trouble with food—bingeing, starving, throwing up. If in your family, you've been the caretaker to a parent in trouble or to your siblings, it may be easy to slip into the caretaking role with the person you worry about. Caretaking can take many odd forms. It may mean not saying something so you won't hurt someone's feelings. It may mean telling someone, when asked, that they look good, even when you don't think so. It may at times mean just looking the other way. Notice what you think caring is—and then ask yourself—is the caring helping? Or is it missing someone who is struggling in front of your eyes?

It is necessary that you distinguish between action that is truly helpful and behavior that comes from your own rules and beliefs about what love looks like. Sometimes your way of caring may actually prevent the other person from getting the kind of help and care that they really need.

THE NEED FOR A SMOKESCREEN

For all of us, often it is easier to worry about someone else than to worry about ourselves. There's no question you are going to worry about the person you love. But how are you expressing that worry? And is it helping the situation? Remember, worry always implies that you don't think the other person is going to be okay. There are times when that may be true and you definitely need to step in. But there are other times when your worry may unwittingly give the other person the message that they can't take care of themselves. As a result, they may quietly feel defeated—or angrily rebel.

Meanwhile it's possible that there is something else important in your life that deserves worrying and attention. Mirta talks about it this way:

> *My husband, Marc, and I had a consultation with my daughter Dorie's therapist last week. The therapist said that Dorie really was doing so much better. She wondered if I had noticed? I know Dorie had been bingeing and throwing up. That's why she went to therapy. But I wasn't*

sure if things were better. I was beginning to get annoyed at the therapist. How was I supposed to know what was going on? Dorie was always so secretive about everything. But then the therapist asked me what I'd be worrying about if I weren't thinking about Dorie. After a long silence and some uncomfortable glances from Marc, I told her that I hated how much my husband drank. I said it so low she didn't even hear me and I had to say it again. I feel like I can only deal with one thing at a time—and the truth is I don't want to deal with Marc's drinking. I can't bear to think I'm living with an alcoholic.

Though Mirta didn't intend this, by not addressing Marc's drinking, both parents were giving Dorie the idea that feelings and worries couldn't be talked about at home. Dorie felt that she wasn't allowed to notice that her dad was passed out on the couch almost every day. Unwittingly, Mirta's attempt at protecting everyone from Marc's drinking gave Dorie the message that eating feelings was better than talking about them.

Substance abuse can be prevalent in the families of people with eating disorders, and frequently a focus on problems with food can hide problems with drugs, alcohol, or other health or body issues that may exist among other family members. This cannot be taken lightly. The person with the eating disorder should not have to take care of their problem before other problems are addressed. If you are someone who has worried (even secretly) about your own use (or your spouse's) of food, alcohol, or drugs, it is possible that a focus on someone else's eating disorder might be keeping you from the business *you* need to attend to. Whenever any questions exist regarding drug or alcohol abuse, 12-step programs such as Alcoholics Anonymous or Narcotics Anonymous (or the sister organizations such as Al-Anon) should be attended for information or a source of support, or a professional should be contacted.

Substance abuse, however, is not the only problem that can be obscured by the focus on an eating disorder. Sometimes, focusing on someone else can distract you from thinking about something in your own life that needs attention. When empty-nester parents focus on an eating-disordered adult child, it means they don't have the time to focus on the next stage in in their lives. A college student whose parents are getting divorced, may find that focusing her attention on an anorexic friend prevents her from feeling sad about what's happening in her own family. A father who directs his anger at a son's bingeing prevents the father from acknowledging his own vulnerabilities and fears.

Eating disorders are tricky. Maybe one of the worst things they do is narrow the experience of everyone involved. There's no question that medical stability is always the first priority, but even in the worst of situations, it is worth taking a moment to ask about who has gotten lost in the face of the difficulties. It isn't always just the person in trouble with food. It often takes time and some consideration to understand what else is needed in our own lives if the focus weren't on our child, our partner, or our friend.

THE NEED TO FILL A VOID

The focus on the eating disorder may make up for something missing in your life. In fact, you may not even be aware that something is lacking. The void may always have existed, or it may be the result of the initial need to focus on someone else to the exclusion of yourself or your other relationships.

Tom was 40 years old when his 13-year-old daughter, Molly, became anorexic. He and his wife, Kathy, 38, spent five years immersed in Molly's problems. They had seen many doctors, followed Molly in and out of residential programs, struggled their way through five painful years of disrupted meals, emotional battles, and the constant fear that their daughter would die. Now it finally looked like the pain was behind them. Molly was settled in treatment and was maintaining a healthy weight. She was able to leave home for the first time and attend college in another state. Kathy and Tom had just received a spirited letter from their daughter. School was fine and it looked like she had even started to date. But Tom remained troubled:

> *I woke up one morning and realized that I was scared to death. Kathy and I had been so involved in Molly's problem that we'd done little else for five years but worry about her. I began to think about how different Kathy and I were—she, so quiet and reserved, and me, outgoing, driven, always involved in something. I thought of how rarely we spent time together these days. We were always in separate rooms of the house.*
>
> *Except for the half-hour around dinnertime, when we exchanged information about Molly and her older brother, who was also away at school, we really didn't have much to talk about. I found myself missing the kids terribly. The house was so quiet now. I got scared that I'd be spending the rest of my life in a dead marriage, just waiting for grandchildren so we'd have something to do.*

What dawned on Tom that morning was how, in dealing with Molly's problems, both he and Kathy had been ignoring their marriage. Something was missing and neither he nor Kathy had wanted to face this. As long as the kids were home—and certainly as long as Molly was sick—Tom had no opportunity to feel the deficits in his marriage. But now that Molly was better and he and Kathy were the only people home, he recognized that his long-standing focus on Molly had allowed him to put off the problems he knew were emerging in his own life.

Tom and Kathy asked Molly's therapist to recommend a family counselor and the two of them began treatment. With the help of the therapist, they began to work on rebuilding their marriage together.

DON'T TRY TO FIGURE IT OUT YOURSELF

The examples we give may feel extreme. They may not apply to your family. But no matter your situation, every family, crisis-burdened or not, can use fine-tuning. Any difficulty in any family can be used as an opportunity for questioning, an opportunity for change. The issues that underlie difficult moments can be multiple and complex. Your own family rules and experiences will color what you think is best. Your child, your partner, your friend will know just what to do to have you respond in old and familiar (even if unhelpful) ways. Change in the way we relate to others is incredibly hard. People committed to the treatment of alcoholics have long known this and, as a result, recognized the need to help the alcoholic's family and friends deal with these issues. Al-Anon was established specifically to help significant others find new ways of relating to the person they loved.

The recognition and need for such support for family and friends is now a part of the treatment of eating disorders. Know that you are not alone with your frustration and the difficulty of knowing how best to proceed.

If you are involved with someone who has an eating disorder, your experience and role may vary wildly. No matter what your experience is, this is an opportunity to be curious—both about yourself and the person with the disordered eating. When a family has a car, the car is usually taken in for a checkup and tuning each year. But when someone has a family, most often, no one takes the family in for a checkup until something breaks down.

When someone you care about is in trouble, there is an opportunity for the kind of fine-tuning that every family or relationship needs. What, besides the eating disorder, needs to be cared for? What needs to be communicated? What needs to be changed? The more you understand about your particular relationship and family, the more likely you are to set the stage for recovery of the eating disorder. But, as importantly, you are also opening the doors for the kind of fine-tuning and change that is necessary in any partnership or parenting situation to meet the ever-growing needs of everyone involved.

9.

WANTING MORE

Relating to the Person, Not the Eating Disorder

THE OVERALL GOAL IS NOT JUST THE ABATEMENT OF DISORDERED EAT-
ing, but the possibility of gaining a clearer perspective on
your relationship with the person you are involved with. It's an
opportunity to explore and resolve frustrations and inequities
in the relationship, and to reestablish and nurture its strengths.

In this spirit, we want to talk about some of the ways to
pay attention to your family and to your relationship. While the
eating issues themselves need to be addressed, it's important
to understand that recovery from an eating disorder does not
have to do with only food. Consider the issues in the following section, think about your relationship or your family, and
question the patterns that have evolved with the person you
care about. Relating to the person, not just the eating disorder,
will best help pave the way for the possibility of recovery—for
everyone involved.

IMPROVING COMMUNICATION

An important part of any relationship is being able to talk
with one another honestly and comfortably. This takes effort.

Equally difficult parts of communication are listening without judging, talking without blame, and allowing oneself to hear the feelings and dissatisfactions of the other without needing to feel like it's a fight.

Learning to communicate takes practice. Many families we see have difficulty allowing vulnerable or negative feelings to be part of the language. This is true in partnerships and friendships as well. Unspoken rules may emphasize that keeping negative feelings to oneself is a virtue or that pretending everything is fine will make things better not worse.

Katherine and Phil Martin were having difficulties with their 14-year-old daughter, Kelly. Katherine told us:

> In our family, we believe that if you don't have something nice to say, don't say it. When Kelly turned 14, she started disagreeing with us about all sorts of things. She raised her voice all the time. This infuriated both of us, but we didn't know how to respond, so we ignored it. Her rage escalated to where she called us names, slammed doors, and broke plates when she was really angry. We knew that she was tortured with feeling fat (her words—she wasn't fat) and that when she was upset, she binged and threw up. She was already seeing a therapist for that, but Kelly didn't want us talking to her therapist. We didn't want to make things worse by calling her.
>
> Finally, Phil and I told Kelly we had to speak to her therapist. Even though the therapist initially wanted to respect Kelly's wish to have her therapy be a safe and private place, we insisted and the meeting occurred. The therapist was really supportive of Kelly, saying that she had a right to be angry. But slamming doors and

vile language were not considered "expressing feelings."
Kelly needed to talk about the differences she had with
us without acting like a possessed demon. We, in turn,
had to learn how to talk more openly and listen to her
complaints.

   The tough part for Phil and me was listening to it
all and taking Kelly's complaints seriously. We've made
some changes. In other places, like curfews, we've stayed
firm. Kelly still gets mad but the horror scenes are defi-
nitely less intense. I guess she was like a pressure cooker,
holding all that back and then exploding.

Matthew, 34 years old, discussed his difficulties communicating with Monica, his 32-year-old wife: "Whenever she's
upset, she cries and then goes and eats. She never gets mad and
really tells me what's disturbing her. It's like a guessing game.
I find myself walking on eggshells with her."

There were many reasons why this couple had trouble
talking with one another, but they had nothing to do with
Monica's eating habits. While Matthew invited Monica to tell
him what was bothering her, he would get angry in response
to her criticisms. And Monica held back for fear of being too
much of a burden to him. She worried he'd leave her if she
complained too much.

The couple needed to spend much time learning what the
other one was thinking and feeling. Monica needed to dare to
speak her mind. Matthew needed to be quiet when Monica
said what she was thinking. No interruptions, no defense—
they each needed just to listen.

Think of your own relationships when someone tells you
something that doesn't seem right. Are you able to stay quiet,

listen, and be curious about what the other person is saying? This is incredibly hard to do—but it's one of the most import- ant guidelines we can give you. When someone has something to say, don't try to defend yourself, don't try to fix it. There will be time for that. Is it possible just to listen?

When an eating disorder is in the picture there is an ad- ditional challenge: to remember that focusing on the eating disorder can interfere with *both* communicating and listening.

GUIDELINES

Here are some general guidelines to keep in mind for improv- ing communication:

- Do not assume someone else's intentions, thoughts, or feelings. Think about how you are feeling and put words to it. Don't say something like "when you throw up, you must be so mad at me." Instead try something like "When you throw up, I feel so helpless that I can't do anything and sometimes I know I get mad."
- Do not blame or attack the other person. Again, talk about how *you* are feeling. Try something like "When you walk in the house and don't kiss me, I feel like you are mad at me. It makes me shut down." Don't just say "You never kiss me anymore."
- Do not say "you always" or "you never."
- If you say "you never kiss me anymore" surely the other person will tell you the one time they did. Then you are in an argument, not a discussion.
- Do not bring up every issue in your relationship that you

are upset about. Stick to the one problem you are discussing.

- Do not induce guilt.
- Don't say things like "We just spent so much money on clothes for you and now you can't fit into anything" or "You spend so much money on Seamless. We need that money for your college." Remember, it's okay to set limits on money or shopping, but increasing the guilt will definitely just make things worse.
- Speak with "I" statements. (See Chapter 4 for a more detailed explanation.) Pay attention; do you even know how you feel? Put words to your own experience, not to theirs.
- Balance your communication. Be sure people know what you like as well as what you're unhappy with. For example: "You've been so much easier around the house. We've been loving spending time with you. But when you come home from school, you go straight to your room and don't even say hi. That feels bad. Can we talk about that?"
- Listen with an open mind, not a defensive one. It's normal to defend oneself, particularly, if you are accused of doing something you don't think you are doing. For example, if your teen says, "You always get mad when I tell you something" *don't* say, "Well, you tell me things that are really upsetting." Just listen! It's likely that some, if not all, of what is being said is true. Make sure you respond when you are calm and—this is the hardest part—try to own even a part of what is being said to you. Maybe, even in the smallest way, something the person is telling you is right.

- Pretend to be the other person. What would they be feeling? What would they want to do or say? Only when you genuinely imagine what it's like to be that person will you be able to seriously consider their concerns and work to make the situation better.

ESTABLISHING RESPONSIBILITIES

In any marriage, intimate relationship, or household, responsibilities are divided. Sometimes what develops works well and feels fair, other times it doesn't.

As we discussed in Chapter 3, in families in which someone has an eating disorder, there may be imbalances in the area of establishing responsibilities in the household. Many times, parents err in one direction or the other, taking over too many tasks for the children or burdening them with responsibilities beyond their capacities. To make matters more complicated, both situations can exist at the same time. For example, teenagers may be left on their own scholastically (even if they are doing poorly in school), while at the same time their parents insist on early and nonnegotiable curfews.

In evaluating the responsibilities with kids, you must realistically consider age and capabilities. Do not work around someone's eating disorder, viewing it as a handicap; this will only discourage them from feeling competent. Helping someone grow up includes allowing increased rights and responsibilities regarding decisions about one's own life (that is, what to wear, what friends to have, what activities to participate in).

Roger and his wife, Patty, grappled with this situation with Cynthia, their 16-year-old daughter, before they were seen in family treatment. Cynthia's eating for several years had been all over the map. While never medically in trouble, Cynthia gained and lost weight, binged and restricted, with a constant focus on food and her body. Dad spoke of their situation this way:

> *It was hard for us to think of Cynthia as being 16. She always seemed and acted younger. She'd ask for our help. She was hurting a lot. We really felt bad for her and didn't want to make it harder for her at home so we really wanted to help. But over time, it seemed we were doing the same things for her at 16 that we did when she was four. We knew if we didn't help, we'd be in for a fight and it just didn't seem worth it. Cynthia didn't even clean her own room—we did. I think quietly (and sometimes not so quietly), Patty and I were walking around pretty mad at her all the time.*

What this family needed were rules that insisted on the daughter's being responsible around the house, rules that weren't determined by the eating disorder. That of course brought in the issue of consequences—and Mom and Dad's worry that it wouldn't be worth the predictable fights.

But with support, Cynthia's parents worked out a system in which she was given a weekly allowance. If household responsibilities weren't kept, her allowance was decreased. Cynthia's room was her responsibility. She could keep it as neat or as messy as she wanted but the rest of the house needed to be kept clean. This was common property and Cynthia had to pitch in. Trash needed to be taken out nightly, the dog walked, dishes cleaned.

Here, no longer did Cynthia's difficulties define how she was to be treated. Roger and Patty had to brace themselves for

Cynthia telling them that she didn't feel well—that she couldn't do what was asked. They had to be braced for her feelings—and theirs. But rules did change and consequences were set up. Cynthia still had to grapple with the hard work of recovery, but no longer was the eating disorder determining how she was to be treated at home in terms of what would be expected of a teen her age.

We see so many families where rules around responsibilities or money are just never made. Kids tell us they know they are pushing the limits but it doesn't really matter. Parents walk around mad. Tracking money and responsibilities is a huge pathway to noticing where things have become problematic. With Cynthia's family, the new rules gave Cynthia more responsibilities, which gave her the message both that her parents were paying attention and also that they felt she was capable of taking care of herself. Even though, at first, Cynthia didn't like this at all, over time, there was much less anger day to day. The old ways of relating clearly had to be shaken up.

In order for change to occur in any relationship, you must be willing to evaluate and balance how decisions are made and how responsibilities are shared.

GUIDELINES

Here are some guidelines for improving the balance of responsibilities in your relationship, even when an eating disorder is in the picture:

If you are parents, look at the rules your family has regarding responsibilities. When children or teenagers are involved, you must make sure the responsibilities are appropriate to their age. If there is disagreement between parents and children, parents ultimately set the rules—but not without hearing their child's opinions. When in doubt, speak with other parents or professionals to establish reasonable expectations.

Between adults, be sure the division of responsibilities is fair and appropriate for everyone involved. Each person's responsibilities should be clearly spelled out so nothing is assumed or taken for granted. Do not minimize responsibilities if someone has an eating disorder.

If there are areas of disagreement, either a household meeting or a planned time to talk can provide a forum for discussion. Use the guidelines suggested for communication when you hold these meetings.

Among adults, disagreements with regard to responsibilities should be negotiated openly until a fair arrangement is agreed upon. When difficulties seem insurmountable, professional advice or even speaking with friends can provide helpful guidance.

RESPECTING RIGHTS

Imbalances that exist regarding responsibilities inherently create imbalances regarding people's rights. This may include the right to age-appropriate freedoms, to privacy, and, when a child is involved, the right to be taken care of.

As we discussed in Chapter 3, if the focus is only on the eating problems, these other issues may get missed, complicating the possibility of change.

THE RIGHT TO GROW UP

One problem we commonly see is that when someone who has had an eating disorder at a young age (we are seeing kids as young as eight with eating disorders), as they mature, they are prevented from experiencing the freedoms that would normally be granted as kids grow up. In our previous example, we discussed how Cynthia was not expected to assume responsibilities typical of a 16-year-old. This was not the only way in which she wasn't treated her age. Her father was nervous about her going out on dates or even hanging around with her friends in the evenings. As a result, Cynthia had to be in by 10 p.m. on weekends. By her parents' standards, this was a fine compromise, but Cynthia ended up feeling like a baby among her friends, all of whom were allowed to stay out until at least midnight.

Part of the work in this family was not only considering responsibilities, but reevaluating rights and freedoms. Having a 10 p.m. weekend curfew was unreasonable for a trustworthy 16-year-old in the community where this family lived. Cynthia's parents were urged to speak with other parents of 16-year-olds to find out what curfews they had for their teenagers. It turned out that many kids were permitted to stay out after midnight.

Cynthia's parents were urged not to evaluate their daughter's rights based on her eating behavior. She was 16 years old, regardless of how or what she ate, and she needed to experience the freedoms that other adolescents her age enjoyed. Her trustworthiness would be based on how she handled these freedoms, *not* on how well she recovered from an eating disorder.

THE RIGHT TO BE TAKEN CARE OF

Rights not only have to do with letting a child grow up and become independent, but also with protecting them from having to grow up prematurely. A child or teenager has a right to be able to depend on their parents to be there as sources of authority, security, and comfort—without having to ask.

In Rayann's situation, she and her mother were very close. Her mother, Susan, was very caring and worked hard to provide a good upbringing for her only daughter. Rayann's parents had divorced when she was three and neither she nor her mother had seen her father since. Rayann, now 14, had been a healthy kid, did well in school, and was very involved socially with a group of friends whom Susan liked and respected. But some months ago, it became clear that Rayann was throwing up. This was the only clue that something might be wrong. Once again, Susan took hold as a caring mom. She got Rayann into treatment and she joined a mothers' group because she wanted to know what to do to help.

Susan describes the outcome of the meetings this way:

> *Rayann and I always have been close. We talk about everything. I always thought this was a good thing, but in the group, they told me that maybe I had become more of a friend than a parent.*
>
> *The group helped me notice how much I depended on Rayann to be there for me. I never thought this was bad, but the group felt that there were certain things I shouldn't be talking to her about, like how I felt about men and sex, how lonely I was, how much her father had let me*

down. Not that I should be phony, they told me, but just
that these were adult issues and could feel burdensome to
a teenager.

Susan was urged to stay in the group in order to develop a support network beyond her daughter. As Susan was able to depend on her peers instead of Rayann, she noticed a burden was lifting from her own shoulders. While she had enjoyed her closeness with her daughter, she had also often felt shaky; after all, relying on a 14-year-old is not a secure position for an adult to be in. With a newfound source of support (the group) and newly felt experiences of security, Susan noticed that she was enjoying her daughter in a different way. She didn't expect as much from Rayann anymore. And she noticed that Rayann seemed to feel relieved. In fact, it seemed she was turning to her mother more these days with her own questions about guys, school, and clothing. For the first time, Susan felt confident about being a mother, not a peer, to her 14-year-old.

Because Susan sought help in response to the signs of bulimia instead of just trying to change Rayann's eating, she was able to work on the areas in her relationship with her daughter in which she could effect change and be of help.

Because kids like Rayann are so quick to fill in and do the jobs asked of them, it is easy to miss how deprived they may feel inside. While they may be very needed and important to their parents, they can also be suffering from neglect that no one sees. Often, because these kids are so responsible and competent, it is easy to miss how in need they are of parents' time and comfort. When this is the case, their rights as children or adolescents are being overlooked.

THE RIGHT TO PRIVACY

Being close in a relationship means allowing the other person privacy. With Rayann, that meant that mom needed to be more private regarding what she talked about with her daughter. In other relationships or families, privacy may literally mean time alone.

Sometimes, time alone may be seen as an insult to other household members or a signal that something is wrong, as opposed to a natural developmental or personal need. If in your family love is measured by involvement and time spent together, you may have trouble establishing privacy for yourself or allowing it for others.

"I remember the first time we decided to shut our bedroom doors at night," said Marlene, a school administrator in her 40s:

> We had been leaving them open since our girls were babies, and somehow it never changed. Now our daughters are 14 and 16. Our oldest, Lydia, protested all along about this open-door policy, but we found it hard to make the change. Somehow it seemed safer to us to leave the doors open. Our support group, however, had a different view and felt strongly that Lydia needed her privacy. After years of being anorexic, she was finally at a healthy weight and was actively struggling to feel more grown-up, and the group felt we needed to support that. At first, I felt that it was unsafe to have Lydia close her door. It was only last year that we thought we had to hospitalize her. I know she's eating now but what if she were exercising in

*her room? What if she were throwing up? I wouldn't hear
it at all. The group reminded me that Lydia still had a
team paying attention to her weight and well-being. They
insisted that I treat her according to her age, not according to my fears.*

*We decided to try it. That first night I lay in bed lis-
tening to the silence of the house. Oddly, my children felt
so far away from me. My husband's steady breathing only
made me feel more alone. I thought how crazy this was,
that just a shut door could make me feel this way. I think
it's the first time I realized that maybe I was having a
hard time letting them be on their own.*

It is extremely hard to begin to give someone privacy and
freedom when they have spent years either secretly throwing
up, exercising, restricting—or certainly if there was a point
when you worried if they were even going to survive. You may
have spent years involved with treatment teams, coaches, and
residential care, doing anything you could to make sure the
person you love regained their health. You've gone through really frightening times.

Yet with any eating disorder, once medical stability is
steady, once the person is out of physical trouble, a critical part
of recovery is for that person to have agency over their own life,
to realize that they are taking care of themselves because they
want to, not because they are complying with a treatment plan
or parental rules. This means that as a part of the work, you
will need to pull back, hold tight and wait to see how and if
the person you love is able to keep the work of recovery going
on their own. Sometimes this means someone leaving home
before you think they are ready. Other times it means allowing

them to eat on their own or, yes, to have privacy in their rooms. Having a trusted professional in the picture can allow for reassurance that someone is paying attention (and indeed you need the reassurance that if there is the start of a relapse, you will be told). Know that if someone begins to slip in the face of more independence there are a myriad of ways to recognize that—change in moods, weight, eating, and so on—even with closed doors.

The person challenged with the eating disorder is not the only one who needs privacy. Every individual has that right, including parents. Peggy, a 42-year-old stockbroker, talked about trying to work during her 18-year-old daughter Jane's struggle with anxiety and bulimia:

> *It seemed as though every time I turned around, Jane was calling me. Sometimes she'd call 10 times a day. I felt so guilty if I didn't talk to her, but my stomach would tighten and I could feel my anger as soon as I heard her voice on the other end of the line. It was becoming impossible to do my job and to be a mom at the same time. I decided to call Jane's therapist to see what to do. Jane was mad, but the therapist suggested that I attend a session and that we all brainstorm how to handle Jane's calls. We came up with the following plan: I set aside time every day when I would talk to Jane outside of work. She lives with me, so we could easily arrange time when I wasn't working. I told Jane that if she wanted to talk to me, we could have breakfast together every morning at 7:30. I didn't care whether she ate, but I wanted her to sit with me. Of course Jane didn't like that idea at all. "No way am I getting up that early to talk to you," she said.*

We also agreed that she could call me once during my lunch hour between 12:00 and 12:15 p.m. and once after the market closed. In the evenings, I'm home. If Jane were home and wanted to speak to me, we could talk then.

If Jane called me at any other time, I was to say I'd speak to her at our next arranged time and then hang up—or I could even just text that to her. I was to do that no matter how many times she called—or after saying it once, I would just not answer. This way, I was available to her, but not controlled by her. Her therapist suggested that during these times, she could write down her feelings and speak to me about them later. Or she could bring them into the sessions to discuss there. Then Jane wouldn't feel that she was just being dismissed.

We all tried these things out. The first two days were miserable. Jane of course didn't wake up for breakfast, she never called me during the arranged times, and she certainly didn't write anything down. Instead she would call at other times, with messages that this time it was urgent. It was hard not to respond. However, after two days of my insisting she call at the arranged times, she slowly started following the schedule. It's now been three weeks and she occasionally calls when she's not supposed to, but I keep to the schedule. There are days now that she doesn't even call at all.

Now that this schedule is working out, I still worry but I'm not walking around angry at Jane all the time.

For any of you reading this book, it is important to think about your own rights—your right to privacy, independence, and time on your own. Parents and couples need time together, separate from their children. Partners need time with friends. And everyone needs time alone to think about what is needed in one's own life. This often is impossible when someone in the family is in crisis. How can you go out to a restaurant alone if that means your child won't eat anything for dinner? How can you go on a weekend trip away if your partner binges and throws up every time you leave? How can you tell your room-mate who has been tormented by weight and food that you need some time with another friend?

No question, there are many situations in which parental presence is critical in order to allow for re-feeding, medical recovery, or the maintenance of stability. In these cases, a treatment team or strong support network should be at your side to guide the way.

But there are many situations where it is much more unclear as to what you should do.

If the person you care about is working on their own self-care, demonstrating signs of attending to what is needed in recovery, this may be a time to think about what you need in terms of your own private time, with your partner, with friends, or on your own. If you are finding that the care you are giving leaves you feeling resentful, furious, or even depressed, that is a sign that it's time to think about you.

Even in the most challenging of situations, consider what other options are available. One important possibility that has developed in the field in recent years is that of therapeutic in-home support programs in which a food coach helps establish, support, and directly monitor meals. Usually food coaching involves in person, on-site direct work, taking over the re-feeding work with the person in trouble. Meal plans are established and literally, bite by bite, support with meal plan compliance is directed and supported. In this time of COVID-19, many innovative techniques have arisen using videos, pictures, and telecommunication to allow for support and monitoring without actual in-home visits. By the time you are reading this, there's no question that support in the field will have evolved even further. But either as a temporary alternative to draw on in certain circumstances, or as a planned, ongoing part of the recovery, food coaches can provide relief when and if that is needed.

The point here—indeed the point of this entire book—is to recognize that if your needs are not attended to, you are not going to be in the best position to support the person in trouble with food. If you are not healthy (emotionally, physically, mentally), you are not going to be able to help the person who is at your side. Ensuring this can take many forms: a regular parental date night; a day when a partner, other caretaker, relative, or food coach gives you a day away from the heated mealtimes; or even, if possible, a weekend away to recharge and stay healthy.

Be thoughtful about what you need—and what you need to make it happen. Get advice from the therapeutic team or support system, but don't forget to take care of you.

GUIDELINES

Here are some guidelines to help you ensure that everyone's rights are being respected in your relationship:

- Individuals in a household have a right to private time and to closed doors. If there is a question regarding whether privacy will result in symptomatic behavior, speak to a professional or support group to help guide the way.

- If you are parents establishing ground rules for your children, independence should be commensurate with age. Check with other parents in your area to see what curfew times are considered reasonable, how much allowance is considered fair, and what other rights and freedoms are granted.

- A child should not be treated as a friend nor as someone beyond their years. Do not tell your child your marital or sexual problems. If you are doing so, you must *stop*.

- Children have differing needs in terms of their parents' time. If your child or teenager is complaining that they do not have enough time with you, listen carefully. They may be right. This may be a point in their life that, even despite being older, they need you there. If this is the case, be sure to make that time happen.

- Establish clearly what times or areas are off limits to others when it comes to phone calls and visits. And establish times when you *will* be available. For example, while the workday is off limits, you might want to make it clear that you will be home for dinners or available to talk during your lunch hour.

- Couples need time alone without children, friends, or relatives. If you find that you and your partner do not spend enough time alone, set up a plan to have dinner or to go out by yourselves. If you have difficulty doing so, it may be time to talk to get outside guidance to help you know what is best to do.

- And no matter what your relationship is with the person you love, make sure to get the time you need, with friends, with your partner, with other family members, and with yourself.

STRENGTHENING YOUR RELATIONSHIPS: WHO IS MISSING FROM THE ROOM?

All of us are like kaleidoscopes. There are endless parts to who we are, how we present ourselves, and how we experience the world. When someone has an eating disorder, they and everyone in a relationship with them gets stuck on one picture—and that picture is often dark. The person suffering from an eating disorder might get stuck looking like a belligerent, enraging, or helpless child or partner. The picture of you, as someone who cares about them, might be of a dictator, a nag, or annoying cheerleader. The myriad of beautiful, exciting, glittering images in the kaleidoscope, the many other parts you both care about, have been forgotten or lost. This happens in any relationship. Patterns develop in unspoken ways that protect the relationship but unwittingly break it down. A critical part of recovery is for everyone involved to notice those patterns—to remember and nurture parts of the person and the relationship that are no longer in the picture—both in the person you care about and in yourself as well. This brings us to the last rule.

FIND THE PARTS OF THE OTHER PERSON—AND THE PARTS OF YOU—THAT HAVE MOMENTARILY GOTTEN LOST

"Things were different before my husband and I got married," said Georgette, 33, about Kevin, 38:

> Everyone loved being with Kevin—especially me. But once we got married, it seemed like I forgot some of that.

He would get me so angry because he was always eating or thinking about food. He gained over 30 pounds after we got married. I was really worried about how much junk he'd eat and we started to argue about that all the time.

Things got bad between us. We finally saw a couples' therapist. She noticed that I was the one in the relationship who was supposed to keep things in order, Kevin was the one who added fun to the mix. That was likely why we had been drawn to each other, but now we were in a pattern where we were keeping each other stuck. All I saw in Kevin was someone who was out of control. All he saw in me was the ever-rigid schoolmarm. How could we break up the entrenched entanglement we were in? How could we remember why we fell in love?

Maybe what started to turn was the day we decided to try to do something fun. Kevin had made a point of setting up a fun afternoon. I, in turn, made a vow to shut my mouth about the eating and just enjoy what we planned to do.

It wasn't so easy getting off the food police squad. I started to notice how much I worry all the time. We went to Coney Island, something we had done on our second date, something I had loved. When we got there, Kevin was so easy and filled with laughter. And me—I was worried about whether he was going to eat hot dogs and cotton candy. Had I become afraid of just letting go?

It's been interesting. I thought the whole problem was Kevin but now I see that I may not be so easy, either. It's not that I'm not still mad about Kevin's eating, but I'm trying to back off more. Kevin has noticed too and (maybe I'm wrong or maybe it's just to please me) but I actually think he has begun to pay attention more. I noticed he hasn't overdone it with food these last weeks. Maybe we both really have needed to change.

There is only one basic guideline to strengthening your relationship and that is:

Remember that there are many sides of you and the person you care about. Do all you can to turn the kaleidoscope and find the pictures that are missing from you, the person you care about, and your relationship itself.

This guideline may be the hardest because in every relationship, people get into patterns that are based on rules that are unspoken but that are meant to keep connection and safety. These rules might be holdovers from one's own family or they may be attempts to do exactly what your own parents didn't do. Kids have unspoken rules of relating that are also meant to keep connection or protect one's self. (For example, it may well be easier to binge, throw up, or restrict than it is to get mad at someone and risk the disruption in the relationship).

We meet so many people—patients, parents, and partners alike—who easily can get mad and express anger, but don't show their vulnerabilities. Often, it's much easier to be furious with someone than it is to realize you are scared. What may be missing is a more tender but certainly less protected part of you, or you may be pleasing, trying to make sure everything is going well, that the other person is okay. Here, it may well be the angry side of you that has no voice.

We all present certain sides of ourselves at different times and in different relationships. Pay attention to the relationships you are in, particularly with the person struggling with food or weight. What part of you do you lead with? What part is missing? And what about the person you care about? What parts of them do you see and respond to the most? Finding the missing parts of yourself or of the person you care about is often really tough. But it is a critical part of recovery—for everyone involved.

ON THE ROAD TO RECOVERY: BOTH THEIRS AND YOURS

Someone struggling with an eating disorder likely has a long road to recovery. Eating disorders of all kinds require an attention to physical health, food, and often medical stability. But there is much more to the person and to your relationship than the food and weight. Paying attention to your relationship, thinking about communication, privacy, boundaries, and growth need to be part of the treatment process. Exploring and potentially changing these parts of your relationship can make a big difference in setting the stage both for sustained recovery, connection, and growth in your relationship, no matter what stage of the process you are in.

This is an opportunity to fine-tune your relationship and to provide a strong base from which everyone can grow and change. We have provided you with tools to help you in your efforts. Professionals and support groups can be your guides.

Don't go it alone, be patient, and learn to discover the ways in which you and the person you care about can get to know each other again.

This is not an easy task. But if you continue in your efforts, there is much possibility for the future.

Remember that hope and love and courage can allow for change, often more than any treatment program in the world.

Notes

CHAPTER 1: WHAT YOU SEE: THE BEHAVIORAL ASPECTS OF EATING DISORDERS

1. Ackard, D. M., J. K. Croll, A. Kearney-Cooke. "Dieting frequency among college females: Association with disordered eating, body image, and related psychological problems." *Journal of Psychosomatic Research* 52 (2002): 129–136.

2. CBS News, "Survey: 97 percent of women have negative body image," CBSNews.com, March 2, 2011.

3. Pope Jr., H. G., , D. L. Katz, and J. L. Hudson. "Anorexia nervosa and "reverse anorexia" among 108 male bodybuilders," *Comprehensive Psychiatry* 34, no. 6 (November–December 1993): 406–409.

4. McClain, Z., and R. Peebles. "Body Image and Eating Disorders among Lesbian, Gay, Bixexual and Transgender Youth." *Pediatric Clinic of North America* 63, no. 6 (December 2016): 1079–1090.

5. Goeree, M., J. Ham, and D. Iorio. "Race, Social Class, and Bulimia Nervosa," IZA Discussion Paper No. 5823, Available at SSRN: https://ssrn.com/abstract=1877636.

6. Swanson, S., S. Crow, D. LeGrange, J. Swendsen, and K. Merikangas. "Prevalence and Correlates of Eating Disorders in Adolescents: Results From the National Comorbidity Survey Replication Adolescent Supplement," *Archives of General Psychiatry* 68, no. 7 (July 2011): 714–723.

7. Kilpatrick, M., C. Ohannessian, and J. B. Bartholomew. "Adolescent Weight Management and Perceptions: An Analysis of the National Longitudinal Study," *Journal of School Health* 69 no. 4 (October 9, 2009): 148–52.

8. Perez M., A. M. Kroon Van Diest, H. Smith, and M. R. Sladek. "Body Dissatisfaction and Its Correlates in 5- to 7-Year-Old Girls: A Social Learning Experiment," *Journal of Clinical Child & Adolescent Psychology* 47, no. 5 (September–October 2018): 757–769.

9. Stice, E. and C. Bohon. "Eating Disorders," In *Child and Adolescent Psychopathology, 2nd Edition,* edited by Theodore Beauchaine and Stephen Linshaw (Hoboken, NJ: Wiley, 2012).

10. V. Boraska, C. S. Franklin, et al. "A genome-wide association study of anorexia nervosa," *Molecular Psychiatry* 19 (2014): 1085–1094.

11. F. E. Smink, D. van Hoeken, and H. W. Hoek, "Epidemiology of eating disorders: Incidence, prevalence and mortality rates," *Current Psychiatry Reports* 14, no. 4 (2012): 406–414.

12. National Eating Disorders Association. "Statistics & Research on Eating Disorders," (n.d.). https://www.nationaleatingdisorders.org/statistics -research-eating-disorders.

13. Ibid.

14. L. M. Donini, D. Marsili, M. P. Graziani, M. Imbriale, and C. Cannella. "Orthorexia nervosa: A preliminary study with a proposal for diagnosis and an attempt to measure the dimension of the phenomenon," *Eating and Weight Disorders* 9 (June 2004): 151-157.

CHAPTER 2: HIDDEN FEELINGS: THE PSYCHOLOGICAL ASPECTS OF EATING DISORDERS

1. Støving, R. K. "Mechanisms in Endocrinology: Anorexia nervosa and endocrinology: a clinical update," *European Journal of Endocrinology* 1, no. 3 (January 2019): 180. See also Berrettini, W. "The Genetics of Eating Disorders," *Psychiatry (Edgmont)* 1, no. 3 (November 2004): 18–25.

2. Steiner-Adair, c., and L. Sjostrom. *Full of Ourselves: A Wellness Program to Advance Girl Power, Health, and Leadership* (New York: HarperCollins, 2013).

3. Steiger, H. "Eating disorders and the serotonin connection: state, trait and developmental effects," *Journal of Psychiatry and Neuroscience* 29, no. 1 (January 2004): 20–29.

CHAPTER 3: RULES AND RELATIONSHIPS: THE FAMILY CONTEXT OF EATING DISORDERS

1. Lock, J. and D. Le Grange. *Help Your Teenager Beat an Eating Disorder* by (New York: The Guilford Press, 2005); Collins, L. *Eating With Your Anorexic* (New York: McGraw-Hill, 2004); Bryant-Waugh, R. and B. Lask. *Eating Disorders: A Parents' Guide* (New York: Routledge, 2004).

2. Wonderlich, S. A., et al. "Relationship of Childhood Sexual Abuse and Eating Disorders," *Journal of the American Academy of Child & Adolescent Psychiatry* 36, no. 8 (August 1997): 1107–1115.

3. Field, A., et al. "Peer, Parent, and Media Influences on the Development of Weight Concerns and Frequent Dieting Among Preadolescent and Adolescent Girls and Boys," *Pediatrics* 107, no. 1 (January 2001): 54–60.

4. Stice E., R. P. Cameron, J. D. Killen, C. Hayward, C. B. Taylor. "Naturalistic weight-reduction efforts prospectively predict growth in relative weight and onset of obesity among female adolescents," *Journal of Consulting Clinical Psychology* 67 (1999): 967–74.

CHAPTER 6: NO ONE CAN GO IT ALONE: SEEKING HELP

1. Le Grange, D. and Lock, J. "Family-based Treatment of Adolescent Anorexia Nervosa: The Maudsley Approach." National Eating Disorder Information Center, 2005.
2. Eisler, I., C. Dare, M. Hodes, G. Russell, E. Dodge, and D. leGrange. "Family therapy for adolescent anorexia nervosa: The results of a controlled comparison of two family interventions." *Journal of Child Psychology and Psychiatry and Allied Disciplines* 41 (2000): 727–736.
3. Berkman, N., K. Lohr, C. and Bulik. "Outcomes of Eating Disorders: A Systematic Review of the Literature," *International Journal of Eating Disorders* 40, no. 4 (2007): 293–309.

CHAPTER 7: WHAT TO DO ABOUT THE PROBLEMS WITH FOOD: PRACTICAL ADVICE FOR THOSE DIFFICULT MOMENTS

1. Delistraty, C. D. "The Importance of Eating Together," *The Atlantic*, July 18, 2014. https://www.theatlantic.com/health/archive/2014/07/the-importance-of-eating-together/374256/.
2. Jusiene, R., et al. "Screen Use During Meals Among Young Children: Exploration of Associated Variables," *Medicina* (Kaunas) 55, no. 10 (October 2019):688.
3. Taffel, R. *Parenting by Heart: How to Stay Connected to Your Child in a Disconnected World.* (Cambridge, MA: Perseus Publishing, 2002).

Index

About the Authors

Michele Siegel, PhD, initiated the idea for this book and was cofounder with Judith Brisman of the Eating Disorder Resource Center that served New York City for more than thirty-five years. Michele died in 1993. **Judith Brisman, PhD, CEDS**, was the director of the Eating Disorder Resource Center. She is an editor on the journals *Contemporary Psychoanalysis* and *Eating Disorders*, is on the teaching faculty at the William A. White Institute, and is in private practice in Manhattan. Dr. Brisman is known internationally as one of the first in her field to develop a treatment program for bulimic patients. She has published and lectured extensively regarding the interpersonal treatment of eating disorders. **Margot Weinshel, LCSW**, is a clinical instructor in the Department of Psychiatry of NYU Medical School and has a private practice in New York City.